THE MAKING OF A
MAVERICK

BY MARLO HIGGINS

MOtivational PRESS
LEADERS IN GLOBAL PUBLISHING

Published by Motivational Press, Inc.
1777 Aurora Road
Melbourne, Florida, 32935
www.MotivationalPress.com

Manufactured in the United States of America.

ISBN: 978-1-62865-466-0

CONTENTS

FOREWORD FOR THE MAKING OF A MAVERICK 6

TAKE THE MAVERICK ASSESSMENT 16

MAVERICK CHARACTERISTIC: CLARITY 18
"Clarity clears the clutter."
   MAVERICK MANTRA 22
   "Speak What You Want to See"
   MAVERICK MANTRA 26
   "I am My Own Competition"
   MAVERICK MANTRA 30
   "You get What You Focus on"
   MAVERICK CASE STUDY 36
   James D. Klein, Executive Vice President, Chief Lending Officer
   MAVERICK ACTION 41
   Four Key Words that define Actions with Clarity
   MAVERICK ACTION 45
   Write an essay on 'what money means to you'

MAVERICK CHARACTERISTICS: ACTION & PERFORMANCE 48
"Actions are the fundamentals of performance and achievement."
   MAVERICK MANTRA 53
   "Systems = Performance"
   MAVERICK MANTRA 56
   "If You Educate Properly,
   the Sale Automatically Happens"
   MAVERICK CASE STUDY 61
   Alison Turner, Sales Leader
   MAVERICK CASE STUDY 66
   Carissa Kruse, Founder, Weddings by Carue
   MAVERICK ACTION 69
   Closing the Success Gap
   MAVERICK ACTION 71
   Record yourself during a business high

MAVERICK CHARACTERISTIC: CONFIDENCE. **72**

MAVERICK MANTRA **74**

"Leverage weekly wins to get bigger results"

"Everyone Wants What I have to Offer"

MAVERICK MANTRA **78**

"You Can't Apologize, and You Can't Make Excuses"

MAVERICK MANTRA **82**

"Nothing Gets you Out of Stuck Faster than Documenting Your Own Success"

MAVERICK CASE STUDY **89**

Gabe Erickson, Founder of Flow Media Inc.

MAVERICK CASE STUDY **92**

Craig Montz, Engineer

MAVERICK ACTION **96**

Self-Worth

MAVERICK ACTION **99**

Take the Strength Finders 2.0 Strengths Assessment tool

MAVERICK CHARACTERISTIC: RISK **101**

"Take big actions and perform at your highest level."

MAVERICK MANTRA **104**

"Champions are Motivated by the Dream, and made by their Routine"

MAVERICK MANTRA **110**

"You Can't Try and Fail at the Same Time, It's Impossible"

A LOOK INTO MY MINDSET OF

MAVERICKS AND CHAMPIONS: **114**

MAVERICK ACTION **115**

Sweatshirt | Shower | Pizza

MAVERICK CASE STUDY **119**

Amanda Lund, Brand Storyteller

A NOTE TO FINISH STRONG **123**

THE MAVERICK MOVEMENT **125**

ACKNOWLEDGMENTS **127**

To my constant devotion to the light, in which it protects

I dedicate this book to my boys, all *three* of you, without your continued love and support, and belief in me this book would never have happened.

Never forgetting the invaluable support of my constant flame, AJ your humor and tenacity are immeasurable.

FOREWORD FOR
THE MAKING OF A MAVERICK

There will never be a perfect time in your life to do a great thing. But you could find the perfect person to help you create the time of your life.

Meet Marlo Higgins.

I'll make this short and sweet, Marlo builds Champions. She makes Mavericks who can change the world. It's that simple – because when you find your WHY you can find the way to lead others to make as big an impact as you do. And make no mistake, impact is where Marlo lives, it's who she is. In fact, it's her word for 2017, maybe the word that best describes her journey in this life. This is what Marlo does – and she does it with bravado, with intensity, with a confidence level as large as the day is long and with heart. Always with heart.

Though I have to say, sharing what's on her heart has not always been easy for Marlo, until she met me. Marlo can take others who are trying to reach major goals in life and help get them unstuck. But for a while she was stuck on only showing her bold and beautiful self to the masses, refusing to reveal what lay dormant or the struggles she faced. It was not in her repertoire because she didn't want to give an inch for fear of showing any vulnerability. Yet she has shared with me, because when you share your story the world beats a path to your door. It's the law of attraction and Marlo is a magnet on high. People want to know what makes Marlo Higgins tick and what her trick is to master the champion strategy, to make Mavericks. This book is your insight into Marlo's gifts.

It's actually pretty easy to define how to become a Maverick - the trick is to be like Marlo. The energy, the drive, the planning, the execution, the results and the refusal to accept anything less than *the all* for those she gives *her all*. A student must look to Marlo as their guide, then look in the mirror and make their move to Maverick status.

I've learned what makes Marlo tick. I interviewed her on her own podcast. I've listened to her speak of her challenges, especially with health and the one thing you realize is that there is nothing that will stop her. If there is a human being on this big, blue planet who is going to make it happen no matter what – it's Marlo. And the best part is she's doing it *for you*. Marlo has mastered the Maverick strategy and she's ready to run side-by-side with you to make your dreams a reality and turn your lack of motivation into mountain-moving results. From the time you hear her speak you feel the energy that can only come from someone who defines passion, perseverance and even a dash of patience all rolled into one.

Marlo's title is Chief Inspirational Officer. I found her on Facebook as I searched for someone who already walked-that-walk and talked-that-talk, for I desire to do something very similar, to be like Marlo. We scheduled a 10-minute call that ended up going for more than an hour. From the first hello I knew Marlo Higgins was a CIO on a mission to change lives.

She's certainly changed mine. She has inspired me to go after my own business – writing, speaking, inspiring. She was right there with me as my motivator and guide as I launched my new Storytelling blog. She was pulling for me and telling me to "let go and create space", as I published my latest book and she is there in any moment when my confidence wanes with a calm, confident air that is a consistent 9.5 out of 10, reminding me I must be the same for others to follow. Lead like a champion, motivate and will myself to Maverick status. You know why? Because there is no other way. Go Maverick or go home.

Live in the past and you're depressed, spend too much time thinking about the future and you're anxious, but live in the present, where Marlo lives, and you're at peace. For all her fire and fury and laser focus on her clients and their challenges, Marlo brings peace to the process.

Remember there's never a perfect time to do a great thing – but time with Marlo means your time will be great, your plan will be perfect, (or at least perfectly planned), your results will lift you to Rockstar status and you will create the life you can be proud of. Marlo's pride in you and your results is reason enough to celebrate. But don't go too high and don't drop too low – for the lessons and the journey is a constant and those strategies taught by Marlo are meant to last a lifetime.

When all is said and done and I think of the center, the soul of Marlo Higgins and her purpose – a song comes to mind - Steve Winwood's *Higher Love*. The lyrics bring Marlo into pure focus for me, and once you get to know her, for you too:

Think about it, there must be higher love.
Down in the heart, or in the stars above.
Without it, life is wasted time.
Look inside your heart, I'll look inside mine.

Life's about love. Living is giving. Marlo is giving you what's in her heart, it's *higher love* - the ability to help you see yourself in all of your infinite possibilities. Marlo is your guide to make your life all it can be, so that you can give the world what Marlo already knows is possible for you.

You are a Maverick. You need only believe it to be true. Marlo Higgins will show you the way.

In gratitude,
Mark Brodinsky

It takes a lot of confidence to act on our desires. I share a sprinkling of Maverick mantras that you can speak and Maverick actions that you can take to get yourself out of stuck and into immediate action all while fueling your self-esteem, self-worth, values, talents and more to make an impact in the world.

I've created simple strategies (through my personal experiences) and turned them into easy and memorable 'Maverick mantras' to take action on to achieve results. They will help you 'move-the-needle' towards performance and assist you in getting out-of-the-way-of-yourself, by clearing away self-doubt.

Throughout this book, I am going to share with you the key fundamentals that I've witnessed in building Mavericks and Champions through: clarity and vision, action and performance, confidence and risk, and telling real stories about these champions and how they utilized these mantras to achieve their definition of success to move upwards to Maverick status.

These actions are the fundamentals that I see that determine where a person falls on the performance spectrum.

On this spectrum, I've created three benchmark levels of performance that I refer to as;

1) MAVERICKS

Mavericks are at the top of their game, but they still have a desire and a drive to move forward, to do more, to achieve more, and to be more. They seek bigger visions of the possibilities and 'what if's' for themselves and others. I've found that Mavericks tend to seek recognition, inspiration and validation. They're pretty confident to do-it-alone but they're also smart enough to know that they've got to 'check-in' with themselves and others to stay on a path to higher levels of performance and achievement.

2) CHAMPIONS

Champions have a strong desire to move up in rank and improve but don't know how; or they don't have a clear plan and they are seeking clarity to the types of actions necessary to move ahead or move up in rank. Most of us fall within this category. We've overcome being a player, but we've not yet arrived to Maverick performance status.

3) PLAYERS

Players are awesome, we need them on the team to complete us. What defines players, is that they are pretty comfortable where they are on the bench. They may choose to settle and not move forward or improve. They've found a comfortable place within their performance level. Players occasionally dwell and may want to quit (either on themselves or their actions). Finding improvement is a struggle.

I think you'd agree that there's a little bit of all of these components in each of us. We've all found ourselves within each of these areas as we've looked to improve, get ahead and move forward in our careers and in life. That's the cool part, we don't have to stay in a certain area of performance, we can choose to improve ourselves or pull back and settle. There is no judgement here just clarity to the types of positions on the team that we are choosing, is everything. And hey, it's cool too if you choose not to accept Maverick status, it's not for everyone. Don't think that you have to get all the way to the top of your performance game or achievement level to be important or have value. We're all important, we all have a role to play on the team. It's really more about managing the expectation you have of yourself. Getting clear that different levels of performance can and do exist and choosing where you want to be is where the value is for you. We're not all seeking to arrive at our highest levels of performance, sometimes we've found ourselves there and find that a lower rank of status actually serves us better. That's ok. This is about you and the value that you bring to the world through your talents, gifts, insights and wholeness. No one is saying you need to be a Maverick, it's more about knowing that the choice exists and if there is a way that we can help you arrive to that status, then hey, we've done our jobs.

THOUGHTS, MINDSET AND MEDITATION

Through my many conversations, meetings, connections, podcast interviews and interactions with high-level visionaries and thought leaders, it's been made clear to me, things are changing. We will be called on in a much bigger way to become braver, be more independent, and we'll have to rely on ourselves to make bigger decisions. Now's the time to develop yourself to a higher level so you're equipped with the confidence needed to react and accept things with a powerful mindset of beliefs to continue and achieve through adversity. Life will happen, we all know that. When I say 'life', I mean disappointments, failures, grief, doubt, and all those things that come with them.

Position, and be prepared to leverage yourself in the most unique and valuable way through mindset, thoughts and introspection. Self-reflection and going within, "looking behind the curtain", as Mark Brodinsky with the Huffington Post said during our podcast interview, is one of the most important actions you can take.

It's these times of powerful reflection and inner searching that allow us to truly tap into our natural gifts, talents, and peace we have within. Go deep, find that inner peace. When I started a daily meditative practice it changed everything. Meditation is the action that I go to when I need clarity. Meditation is the ability to shut out distractions and allow oneself to receive inner guidance. This will help you through the tough times. This is where the answers are found; within you.

Meditation is how I start each day. If I'm asked, "what are two words that best describe you", they would be; *grounded* and *consistent*. This meditative practice feeds that grounding nature. When I'm interacting with clients, I'm giving it my all. Meditation allows my body to give back to itself.

I'm described as a motivational force, I'd agree with that. I joke that it takes a tsunami of actions to get things to happen, I guess I'm that force that ignites power within (for my clients). It takes just as much force, to slow me down. This is what meditation is for me.

Introspection;

in·tro·spec·tion

The examination or observation of one's own mental and emotional processes.

"quiet introspection can be extremely valuable"
Self-analysis, self-examination, soul-searching, self-observation.

I invite you to look inside and challenge yourself to bring out your best, pull it forward through meditative action and introspection to get the insights needed to achieve. You matter. Take the time to learn who you are and what makes you tick; what allows you to overcome rejection or difficult times and position yourself to win.

Mavericks don't give in, they don't give up. They wake every day with a 'fire-in-their-belly' and know that they are their own competition. They have to compete only with themselves. When we take on the task to perform at our highest levels and improve what we can, we win. Everyone wins around us when we do this.

WHY DO OUTCOMES OR RESULTS MATTER?

Results and outcomes allow us to gain confidence, when we're confident we become better at leading ourselves and ultimately others.

When we do this, we perform at higher levels. When we perform at higher levels we do more, we achieve more, we become more.

This is what I refer to as a Maverick. Mavericks achieve results. They are at the top of their game. They give it all they've got to improve and remove fear and doubt. They rely on themselves to figure it out, to find a way to overcome the obstacles and barriers they may experience. Mavericks go over, under or around the walls that block them from achievement. It's this relentless pursuit of the goal that keeps them moving. However hard it may be to move, they know they deserve it and they have that burning desire to make it happen.

WHAT'S THE POWER YOU RECEIVE WHEN YOU BECOME A MAVERICK?

The Power of Performance. When you perform at your highest levels, you have a greater understanding of your self-worth, which naturally increases your overall self-esteem.

Your self-esteem matters because it's the foundation of your inner-confidence, your ability to see things through, your strength to never-give-up (on yourself or your dreams). You achieve.

Self-worth (aka self-esteem) = YOU

Confidence = The purity of actions produced by a mind free of doubt

Confidence fuels Performance

Performance fuels Achievement

This is the making of a Maverick.

We build Champions in Business and in Life. – this is my souls purpose.

We build Mavericks by developing a Champions Mindset for Performance.

You can already hear how powerful these Maverick mantras will be for you when you start to implement them.

You're a champion, you're motivated and you have a dream, you just need to script the routine, be consistent and gain the confidence to get there.

As Your Chief Inspirational Officer (CIO), I work with you to honor and allow. A very different approach from trying and forcing things. You'll step into that space which opens up opportunities to thrive, feel peaceful and on-point and stand taller.

You've got it. You can do this.

"Champions are Motivated by the Dream, but made by their Routine"

– Marlo Higgins

This idea of finding commonalities in successful people has blossomed into a mission for me. I look for Mavericks, those that are willing to do what others are not. Those that embrace the process. Mavericks operate in a way that's so consistent they can be studied. The purpose of this book is to share that process with you.

In the following sections I will introduce you to six individuals who have paved their own path to success. In each section you will:

» Learn the characteristic each Maverick exemplifies

» Read notes from each Maverick about their journey

» Learn the mantras they used to help them succeed

» Take an action you can use to achieve your own results

I've formatted the book in this way to be used as a study guide. Read a section, take the action, and write down the results of those actions.

There are also directional guides to links to videos, podcasts, and online articles that act as supporting material. By the end of this practice you should be able to identify at least three things that have changed you for the better.

We come from different places and circumstances, but I know one thing is universally true; everyone starts at zero. Whether you are earning six figures or writing ideas on cocktail napkins, you have everything you need to become a Maverick. Here's the question I pose to you – are you ready to take action?

Love & Belief,

Marlo

TAKE THE MAVERICK ASSESSMENT

My professional experience has been focused on challenging and assisting others to achieve their very best. I see the value each of us has when we understand that we matter. Match that understanding with continued awareness and development; We will move mountains. That momentum is for ourselves and for others, meaning we can take certain types of actions within specific areas of growth that will assist us in performing at our very best, showing us that we can improve if we choose.

The burning love and desire to assist others in seeing their highest value to become a Champion or a Maverick has driven me to create and develop tools and resources that assist in doing just that. Making more Mavericks and Champions in business and in life.

I find power in taking actions. Doing something that can assist us in understanding who we are or what makes us tick, or what's inside of us then how to align this uniqueness and bring that out of us to ensure we serve and perform from our highest level; our perfect source. When that occurs, we become a Maverick.

The Maverick Assessment is just that, an action you can take to assist you in seeing where you are currently on the performance spectrum of Maverick, Champion or Player.

These actions are the fundamentals that I see that determine where a person falls on the performance spectrum.

1) **Clarity**; We all need clarity to understand how to get to where we're going. When we clearly see what we need to do, what direction we need to take, and the actions that will get us there, things start to get easier.

2) **Action**; The words "Action" and "Performance" are often interchangeable. However, there's a distinction you should know;

actions are motions to be completed, but performance requires intention.

3) **Confidence**; Knowing your self-worth means having unlimited confidence to ask for the sale, ask for the salary you desire, ask for the project to oversee, ask to take the lead, to take bigger actions which will produce bigger results.

4) **Risk**; It's when we step out and take a risk that we really find out about who we are or what's inside of us.

Take the FREE Maverick Assessment at www.marlohiggins.com

I know you're busy, but it will take between five to seven minutes to complete. Five to seven minutes is time you do have.

You'll receive scores across the 4 fundamentals that are referenced in the book; Clarity, Action, Confidence and Risk. This assessment will help you see where you are within each of these areas.

Once you complete your assessment you will receive your scores, recommendations and other resources. You're welcome to share that link or your results with your peers or team.

Maverick Characteristic: Clarity

"Clarity clears the clutter."

MAVERICK CHARACTERISTIC: CLARITY

We all need clarity to understand how to get to where we're going. When we clearly see what we need to do, what direction we need to take, and the actions that will get us there, things start to get easier. We stop wondering and actually *start doing* because we're no longer overthinking. Clarity clears the clutter. It may be our cluttered mindset, our cluttered tasks, our uncertain actions. Clarity has power. Without the power of infinite clarity, it's harder to press on.

It's like going through life with a dirty windshield. Think about it... dead bugs, smears, and all that yuck. Its sitting right there in front of you. When you look ahead all you can really see are those dead, smeared and smattered bugs all over the windshield – these are the things that are distracting you from the road. This is what it's like to go through life without clarity. It's harder to see the bigger picture when all you can see are those dead bugs. I invite you today to clean up all those dead bugs. Take the time to stop, use these Maverick mantras as your tools to clean your windshield so you can get back in your car with crystal-clear vision with no barriers or obstacles and be able to look ahead to the bigger areas of achievement. Don't let what's sitting right in front of you gum you up and smear your thinking.

ANALYSIS PARALYSIS

There are often so many possibilities when creating a path to success that people get suck in the "what if" stage, in a process called Analysis Paralysis. In order to take action, we must surrender to the possibility of failure. When we accept the uncertainty of what's coming, we are able to shift our mindset from fear to empowerment. The way we do that is through a process of clarifying what we want for our businesses and ourselves.

Becoming the kind of person, I refer to as a Maverick starts with clarity. Thinking of that goal that's sitting off in the distance? A Maverick doesn't just see the finish line. They create clarity around that goal by working backward, envisioning each step it took to get there until they make it back to the present. By breaking down a goal from *finish to start* we can see exactly what it takes to achieve anything.

Sometimes taking a look at the gap between where you are currently and where you want to be can cause that feeling of overwhelm that keeps you stuck. The way to get beyond that barrier is to give yourself mini "stretch" goals along the way. Here's an example:

Your ultimate goal is to give a TED talk. It's attainable, but not without a strong topic and speaking experience. You decide to start giving presentations to smaller groups in order to strengthen your skills and create awareness around your topic with a goal of one presentation a month.

A way to stretch that goal would be to simply double it. What if you gave two presentations a month instead of one? Would that get you to your goal faster?

Setting these mini "stretch" goals allows you to take action, and stops you from feeling overwhelmed which moves you through any kind of paralysis you may be experiencing. It's this action component and just doing it, that's moving you forward.

One of the first strategies I teach my clients is this: introspection. By having conversations that elicit answers from within, I help my clients get over that initial paralysis by looking in the mirror for solutions to the questions that keep them stuck.

What is it about taking action that stops you? You're looking for the magic bullet that gets you out of stuck, hoping it takes over and gives you all the answers. Well...it's within YOU.

ASK THE RIGHT QUESTIONS

When seeking clarity, it helps to interview yourself and identify exactly what needs to be done to get you to the next level of success.

Write down your answers as if you were responding to an investor who is interested in your business.

» What do you want to achieve?

» What is it about money that is either stopping you or keeping you from getting to the next level?

» What is it about competition that keeps you playing small?

» Do you truly understand what your offering feels like?

» Would you buy from you?

» Would you follow you?

» What's the value of your offering?

» How do you tap into your vision?

» Why is it important to be validated?

» How do you feel when you operate with peace and ease?

» What's the importance of self-recognition?

» What does having clarity truly offer you?

» Action and fear go hand in hand. What's it going to take to remove the fear so you can start taking action?

» When you think about accomplishing your goal, what makes you the most excited?

» What will a clear plan do for you?

» Consistency is King! How can you truly tap into it and keep it alive?

The answers from these questions should give you clarity about what you are trying to achieve. If you find yourself drawing blanks to more than one or two questions, it's time to go back to your goal and determine whether or not it's what you really want to do. Armed with clarity, you will be able to speak about your goals with a new level of certainty and confidence. When you know the how and the why, it's easier to determine the when of your own success.

MAVERICK MANTRA

"SPEAK WHAT YOU WANT TO SEE"

Watch Maverick Video ONE:
Speak What You Want to See

The video that accompanies this Maverick mantra can be found on my YouTube playlist The Making of a Maverick

I frequently work with people who find themselves being very disempowered, not having the confidence that it takes to execute. **"Speak What You Want to See"** Maverick mantra is a great starting point and one that I teach early on, because it allows you to see that you have power and impact that you never realized. When was the last time you considered speaking what you'd like to see and that it could or would actually happen?

When I started showing others to first define what they'd like to see happen, then approach it by stating this fact, it quickly became a game-changer for them. Let me lead by example so you truly understand what I'm saying.

In 2007, I developed a strategy called Successboarding™. Whenever I shared this strategy with others and would show them how to implement it, they immediately saw the value of it. It's a self-recognition strategy that shows you how to document your success, then "speak that success and nothing less", yet another Maverick mantra". You'll learn more about Successboarding™ in the coming pages.

The years went by and this strategy grew, proving itself so frequently that it became a fundamental to most everything I coach regarding confidence. I believe in this strategy so much that I want to share it with more people, so I started the process of trademarking and copywriting, testing it in the marketplace and working with others to keep improving it and enhancing it. Every time I had the opportunity to share it I would always **"speak what I wanted to see"**, what I mean by this is; I would share this comment every time I would introduce the Successboarding™ strategy "someday, this will be a two-minute segment on the Dr. Oz show". I would speak this with such conviction that I could feel it and see it actually happening. I've always told my assistant that someday we'll be on a plane to New York getting ready to be on the Dr. Oz show or on Good Morning America and share this strategy with the world.

By speaking what I wanted to see, the reaction was always; "so, when does the episode air on national television?". Even though it hasn't happened yet, by believing in it so powerfully and speaking with such conviction like I do, utilizing this Maverick mantra, I have no doubt that it is going to happen, it's simply a matter of when.

SPEAK IT, THEN DO IT

I continue to challenge my team with this task of getting us on national television to share Successboarding™ with the world. You can hear how this vision could easily become our reality (if we don't give up on it). Again, I think this is juice for a Maverick. I don't think any vision or idea is too big or too small. If you continue to **"speak what you want to see"** and believe in it forcefully, it will happen. One day the call is going to come and we will be sharing and showing more people what Successboarding™ is and why we believe it's so powerful and the impact it has when you adopt it and start implementing it.

If you've watched the movie Joy, with Jennifer Lawrence, you know what I'm talking about. Throughout her triumphs, Joy created the vision of the mop that went on to sell in the millions, I'm guessing most households have one. If you watch that movie, you'll relate to this strategy. She had this burning desire to develop this mop that would change the way people cleaned their floors. It was so powerful and had such value, that Joy was in the relentless pursuit to make it what she thought it could be. I'm guessing that she may have used this Maverick mantra herself **"speak what you want to see"**, because she was challenged to go on QVC and introduce it. It took conviction and clarity to take that type of action in sharing her mop with the world. It becomes what you believe in, then stating it through this powerful Maverick mantra that allows this strategy to work for you.

WHAT DO YOU WANT TO SEE?

What's going to happen when you shift your speaking and thinking to a mantra like this? You're putting down a foundation and speaking what it is that you want to see happen. This gets others to believe and follow along with you. It's that momentum that keeps your dream going when things go off track. It's imperative to making things happen.

What's an outcome or a goal, you'd like to see? Set it into action by speaking what you'd like, and what you desire to have happen.

When I talk about vision and planting the seeds of possibility with others, it starts by defining the goal then speaking about that goal with clarity and conviction. So much clarity and conviction that the vision becomes your reality. That is what inspiration is; it's your ability to visualize what's possible. You don't have to worry about *how*, that will come, rather be more concerned with *what* you'd like to do and put all the effort towards creating that vision. This vision is what gives us the ability to perform at our highest levels.

MAVERICK MANTRA

"I AM MY OWN COMPETITION"

Watch Maverick Video TWO:

I am My Own Competition

The video that accompanies this Maverick mantra can be found on my YouTube playlist The Making of a Maverick

You Are Your Own Competition. I love this one, because I believe that we all have that interior feeling that we've got to compete with everyone else to win the race. What I've found is this - when you spend that time and energy focused on your "why" instead of what everyone else is doing, everything falls into place.

The difference between being inspired and comparison is most evident in how it makes you feel. Inspiration leaves you feeling hopeful and excited about what you do. Comparison leaves you feeling inadequate and overwhelmed, not knowing how you'll ever accomplish what you've set out to do.

How much time are you spending comparing yourself to others? When we do this, it drains our confidence. As your Chief Inspirational Officer, I challenge you to quit NOW!

Focusing on finding inspiration within yourself and your own environment will allow room for more positive energy and ultimately personal growth. When you're feeling the need to compare yourself to others, here are a few suggestions to find inspiration instead:

GET OUT

Spend time on yourself. Instead of scrolling through your Facebook or LinkedIn page and wishing you had more views or followers, instead, take a walk and reflect on your personal wins and outcomes. You'll find yourself in a larger headspace that makes room for personal growth and strategy, rather than feeling inadequate.

It's so easy to get tangled up with comparison. It breeds fear and so many other negative consequences. When we're comparing ourselves to others it keeps us playing small. Rather, use that fear and release it in a way that others see your strength, confidence, power and substance vs the fear you may be feeling.

Getting out of your own way is getting clear on the areas you need to improve on. Rather than spending time comparing, ask yourself a few questions:

» What areas do you need to improve on?

» If you could change one thing about your approach, what would that be? And why?

Personally, I know that when I enter a room there will be others who may be smarter than me, I'm never concerned with comparison. I've never chosen to focus my energy on intellect, rather I've spent my time on emotional intelligence, being in the people business. Relatability and human emotion is where I've found the most success. I prefer to surround myself with others who I can learn the most from.

I make a conscious effort to reframe my mindset and be open to learning. The faster we let go of comparisons and respect what others have to offer, the more time we have to connect with them. When we give up competing in favor of learning, it changes the energy in the room. Others can sense that we have a genuine desire to *learn* rather than *compete* with them. We all have gifts to share and we all have value. When we focus on our self, the outcome is more about who we are and what we bring rather than achieving someone else's results.

GET A SLOGAN

Wake up and tell yourself **"I am my own competition."** Put this Maverick mantra into action by making a conscious effort to push yourself to that next level. By competing with yourself, you are essentially giving yourself an advantage. In this race, you already know how to beat your challenger. Embrace the feeling of empowerment that comes with knowing you can win. When we take the time to improve the things we need to change within ourselves it opens up a completely new space for power and energy to flow through us.

GET VISUAL

Having a plan in writing helps alleviate that feeling of being overwhelmed that happens when we see others who have achieved goals we're striving towards. I always say "goals not written down are simply wishes". Put pen to paper and script out your plan. You don't have to know all the exact details, but it helps to flush out what's on your mind and map it out onto a piece of paper. Once you've started the first, initial steps, keep at it, use this mapped out plan to get visual and strategize what you desire to make happen. Mavericks are always working on a plan. Mavericks know the value of pen to paper and how to release what their thinking and put it down in writing instead.

After I introduced this Maverick mantra **"I am my own competition"**, with a client, he was astounded how he started thinking differently and immediately people were drawn to his business and services because he was consistently inspired by his own success and how he was more focused on *improving* than *competing*. You can achieve this same result by simply being aware of how much time you focus on *comparing* rather than *being inspired*. Buy back some of that energy you're giving away and step into your own.

MAVERICK MANTRA

"YOU GET WHAT YOU FOCUS ON"

Watch Maverick Video THREE:
You Get What You Focus On/Shiny Pennies

Watch Maverick Video FOUR:
30 | 60 | 10 Formula

The videos that accompany these Maverick mantras can be found
on my YouTube playlist The Making of a Maverick

THE VALUE OF FOCUS AND TIME

In 2005, I was leading a very large independent sales team on a nationwide level. The one key question I was consistently asked was this; 'what should I be doing with my time?'.

Time matters and when you align the time that you have with the right types of actions, you'll have greater results. A lot of this comes down to self-management. I say self-management, because we all have the same amount of time it's really about our self and how we choose to spend our time and the actions we take to ensure our results. It's also empowering when you feel you are in control of your time and choosing which actions to take. When we're empowered, we have greater personal fuel to launch and sustain projects and growth objectives.

WHAT IS PERSONAL FUEL?

It's the way I like to describe our energy. Energy is fuel. This fuel can be described in many ways, it's up to you, but understand that you've got to have it in order to keep going. Think of a rocket and the massive amounts of fuel it takes to lift it off the ground and ignite it into the air. Now, envision this massive amount of fuel that you have within you, that allows you to ignite your rocket and lift off to unlimited heights. We have to have this personal fuel to thrive and survive. When we are depleted and run out, it's impossible to keep going. We've essentially sidelined ourselves because were too busy moving and doing that we didn't pay attention to the fact that our tank is almost empty. This is awareness. Be aware of your personal fuel tank and how it ensures your success. Our personal fuel is when we are fully empowered. We have no limits, we are not tapped out. We are full and ready to launch, and keep our rocket in the air. Be aware when you are starting to feel depleted and no longer empowered. This is your internal guide, **your personal fuel gauge.**

To maximize this fuel, I crafted a formula that has helped hundreds gain clarity to self-management and how they should be spending their time to get the results they are seeking, it's called the **30|60|10 Formula**. In this formula, I've defined three key areas to focus on to ensure you run active and consistent.

They are: Growth, Service and Follow-up.

Growth (spend 30% of your time growing); this is the bloodline to business. I just shared the mantra **You Get What You Focus On**; when you're focused on growth you'll get growth. But first, you have to understand that you need to focus and take actions on growth to get there. One of the reasons we stay in business, is because we're growing, changing, developing and doing.

The easiest way to approach 'growth focus' is to write the numbers 1-10 on a piece of paper, then ask yourself "what are 10 growth actions I can take to grow personally and professionally?"

Once this list is detailed and defined, I invite you to spend two hours a day focusing on one to three of these growth actions. If you spend 2 hours a day, that's 10 hours a week and 40 hours in a month, totally focused on growth. What would happen if you spent an entire week of every month focused on growth? You'd be growing, right?

That's the point. Find clarity around the actions you can take towards growth, and then get to work and take those actions. Look at this list of 10 growth activities as a living, breathing document. You'll want to keep this list nearby as you continually omit and add actions to it.

Let me share an example with you; let's say you write a blog about your business, products, and customer experiences. Spending one hour each week writing your blog, then sharing it on all your social media and marketing structures is a growth activity. It's an action you are taking to share and educate about what you do, how you do it, or the value of it for others. See, this is a growth action. Another action would be networking and getting into the room with qualified folks who could use your services or products. Spend 1-2 hours every day networking your business, and you're growing and gaining exposure. This list is easy once you get rolling creating it. Don't just create it though, print it off, keep it with you and set an intention to take a growth action every day for 2 hours. At the end of the month, look back to this list and omit the growth actions you took that did not produce results and replace them with new actions you can try the coming month. Once this becomes a habit in your business, you'll really start to define your very own personal success formula for how you grow and what you do to make that happen.

Service (spend 60% of your time serving in your craft); this is the easy one. It's doing what you do in business. It's the basics of what you do. I'm a coach, a Chief Inspirational Officer, so when I'm coaching, I'm serving. That's it. So, what do you do in business? Take that action every day for 5 hours a day, that's 60% of your time doing what you do to work your business and serve.

Follow-Up and Follow-Through (spend 10% of your time each day following up); Did you know that there are billions of dollars lost every year because people do not follow-up or follow-through in business? Even worse, they can spend way too much time doing it, eating up valuable work time. Creating a healthy boundary around this action will ensure your success.

Why don't people follow-up? The number one reason is they think they're bugging others when they do. That's such a myth and a poor way of thinking. Rather, look at this follow-up as a touch point and opportunity to *saving them time*, not wanting them to miss out on what you're following up with. Switch that 'bugging thinking' to 'opportunity thinking' and now take the action to follow up with emails, phone calls, appointments or any other actions that you need to take.

Following-up is a clear component to being successful. It shows your integrity and what a good steward you are with your business. You gain respect from others when you do what you said you were going to do.

Create a clear system that allows you an hour every day or 10% of your time following up.

The other reason people don't follow up, is they don't make time for it. Mavericks make it a core fundamental of their systems. Systems = Performance (we'll go into greater depth later in the book on systems), when you implement a clear system like this to grow, serve and follow-up, you win as a Maverick every time.

You can see how simple and clear this 30|60|10 Formula is. 30% of your time is spent in growth mode, 60% doing your job and serving, and 10% following up and following through. This ensures that you spend every day buttoning up your business so you can segway into your evening and end of the week feeling whole, and complete and having total peace and ease. This allows for sustainability as well. Of course, every week is not going to go as planned, heck, every day is not going to, but with clear intentions and clarity of how you're spending your time and in what areas will bring you results, guaranteed.

An added tip; when I mention one hour a day on follow up, this also allows for healthy boundaries in your business. How awesome does it feel knowing you can put off all those pesky emails throughout the day that distract you from producing, knowing that you will return to those during a set time that you've carved out to do so? You've just bought yourself time and production, knowing that you've given yourself an hour to return to those touch points at the end of the day. Ahh this is easy, right?

An added mantra; I coach clients through this strategy and often get asked how many times is appropriate to follow up? The best way to answer this is through yet another mantra **"pursue to a level of professionalism."** Let's say the person you are following up with also lives in your community and you happen to run into them at the grocery store. Completely out of context of being in your business routine, this is off hours and you happen to see them in the bread isle at the market.

If you run the other direction and avoid them, this tells me that your gut is telling you...you've pursued this opportunity too much and it no longer feels professional, rather pesky. But, if you can walk up to them and have an easy conversation and remind them that "hey, I've been trying to connect with you, I've got an opportunity that I'd love to share with you", and it still feels right to connect with them at this level, then you've not yet completed the task of following up effectively with them.

When we operate our businesses authentically while staying accountable for performance levels, we're onto something. Let's say you've called and tried to connect with this person six or seven times without a response, but when you run into them outside of business hours and it still feels good to mention that you'd really like to connect. This is your validator to keep asking. Let this added mantra assist you in knowing when to keep going, or when to let it go and bless and release that prospect and say "next", and move on.

MAVERICK CASE STUDY

JAMES D. KLEIN, EXECUTIVE VICE PRESIDENT, CHIEF LENDING OFFICER

James is one of my fondest client case studies and stories and why I chose to share his first. Working with James Klein, is when it became very evident that I was onto something with this whole Maverick concept. James is a very accomplished professional and through his continued success, he wanted to validate and develop his Maverick status to better understand how to harness his talents and continue to apply them while serving in his industry.

James brought out the best in me too. His openness to learning and being coached inspired me to be vulnerable and share more about myself. His ability to connect with people is why he's such a leader in his industry. It's easy for people to follow James because he's highly relatable and has this ability to bring out the best in others. I've learned a lot being on the receiving end of his wisdom and knowledge through our coaching partnership.

But why did we align and what did we do that allowed results?

In James' words; *"I am what I am."* *Significance. Connecting. Recognition. Influencing.*

James had clarity to what he wanted to accomplish with his time and knew the areas he wanted to develop, that is why he's aligned to the clarity characteristic of Maverick status. Our coaching partnership allowed James to go deeper into strategy and understanding that brought results.

The Maverick mantras that best served James through our coaching partnership were; **"Speak What You Want to See"**, **"I am my Own Competition"**, and **"You get What You Focus on"** – each of these strategies offered James the grounding tools for greater development and success. There were many Maverick mantras shared and coached on, but these were the ones that had the biggest impact for James.

Coaching is about synergy. What we're striving to accomplish can be bigger than us and it takes the synergy of others to challenge, stretch and validate us. That's where our coaching aligned. As I started to position this book, it was important to me to align others' successes to it. I took a variety of clients that I have worked with over the years and asked them to be a part of it, and share (from their vantage point) what they wanted to, which makes for better learning for others. To witness someone else taking action and getting results. That is the value and the reason why I wanted to share real stories and interject others vantage points. It makes our learning and outcomes more powerful.

"I am what I am." Significance. Connecting. Recognition. Influencing.

It only took me 40+ years, but I can honestly say that "I am what I am" and I feel great about that. Working with Marlo has helped me get to this point with so many eye-opening examples and techniques.

When we begin a career, we are influenced and surrounded by other successful people. We quickly notice what they do really well and we also quickly notice what we do not do so well. We try to change who we are and how we do things. It causes internal conflict. I think it is a very natural tendency to focus on what we are not good at instead of what we are good at in life. Most people spend nearly every waking minute trying to improve on their weaknesses or beating themselves up because they are not as good at some things as other people. It really is a shame. It wastes so much time and it causes so much stress. When you truly get to the point where you know who you are and own it—life gets easier. As Marlo says "You have flow" and things seem to come more naturally. The books Strengthsfinder and The Slight Edge led me to a change in how I perceive myself and it has been a tremendous blessing. Prior to meeting with Marlo and reading these books, I spent a fair amount of time trying to "fix" the things that I was not an expert at in my career. It took a lot of work. It caused a lot of frustration. Because of the books, I realized that some things will never be a main strength of mine and that is ok. Instead I could take that effort and pour it into what I am naturally good at and the results have been amazing. Once you realize who you are and how God made you, it makes all the difference. Now I own who I am. Now I am ok with my weaknesses. Now I am a happier person. Now I am able to help others more. It is so rewarding and fulfilling to be who you are meant to be. It is so enjoyable to share your gifts with others and feel good about it. The last few years my career has reached heights I could not have imagined because I have grown comfortable in my skills and talents and worked hard to make them even better. I am convinced that effort invested in your strengths is far more valuable than effort invested in your weakness. Because of Marlo and our work together I am proud to say "I am what I am!"

Once you are "comfortable in your own skin" it frees you up to help others. That is what I love. Everyone wants to feel significant. Everyone wants to feel included. Everyone wants to feel appreciated and valued. Once you appreciate yourself your ability to appreciate others skyrockets. One of my God given talents is Leadership and bringing out the best in people. It comes easily to me and it makes life rewarding for me. I love people. I love being around people. I love mentoring. I love helping people reach their goals and obtain happiness that they might not have imagined being possible. To me, there is nothing more powerful than playing a role in someone's life, big or small, and see that lead them to success. And the wonderful thing is that most times it is the small things that we do that make all the difference. I have found that listening is one of the best gifts I can give people. I think that most people in the world would agree that having a conversation with someone and feeling like they are truly listening is one of the best feelings in the world. It validates you. It sends you a message of significance. It motivates you. To truly feel heard is a wonderful thing. Another small thing that you can do is to value each *person as an individual. Everyone has a story. Everyone has struggles. Everyone has pain. Everyone has joy. Everyone has feelings. Taking the time to connect to people on a personal level makes the difference. And appreciating what makes them unique is so powerful to them and you. Every person has something to offer. Every person can help someone else. Take the time to scratch below the surface of who someone is. Find out what makes them tick. Find out what motivates them. Find out what makes them feel significant. And then do it. Make a difference in their lives. Make a difference in your life. Find ways to catch people doing great things. Every person does great things every day. From holding open a door for someone to smiling at a stranger on the street- every person impacts others. In your workplace, recognize and compliment people for doing "the right things" whether they are big or small. Many times, the big events only come after a series of small events. Every great event has a foundation of items that have been built over time by many people and many small events. Celebrate these small events. Let people know that their kind gesture does make a difference! Make them feel significant.*

A way in which I enjoy helping people is through connecting people. In fact, that is how I met Marlo. I attended a leadership luncheon several years ago and Marlo was one of the panelists. I was so impressed by Marlo and her no-nonsense approach that I picked up the phone and asked her if we could visit over coffee just so I could learn a bit more about her. As they say, "the rest is history", but without me picking up the phone that day...our paths would have likely never crossed. Since they crossed, my life has been enhanced and Marlo has brought me to a higher level of appreciation of who I am and who others are in life. It has brought me a deeper connection to myself and it has helped me connect with others. Once I saw and felt the impact of Marlo on me, I knew I wanted to connect her with others. Since that initial coffee, I have proactively connected many people to Marlo. Some are people I work with and some are community connections. I want people to have that cup of coffee with Marlo and see how she might fit in their lives. I love connecting people. Both people usually benefit. And I feel good knowing that I brought two people together that may never have met otherwise.

The final thing that I have come to understand and appreciate more due to my meetings with Marlo is the concept of "Influence". I have learned that influence means so many different things to so many different people. I believe that everyone wants to feel that they have influence over something. The trick is finding out where their talents intersect with their ability to influence. Some people influence by leading people. Some people influence by how they talk. Some people influence by how they carry themselves. Some people influence by telling stories. Some people influence by listening. Some people influence by smiling. In my work with Marlo, I have discovered so many ways that people can influence. And I have had the courage to proactively visit with coworkers about how they can best influence with their talents. Society teaches us that power and position is the way to influence people. And sometimes it certainly does. However, for many people, power and position is not where their talents are best served. Finding how people can influence most naturally has been an exciting journey as I meet and mentor people. So many people that I have mentored are happier in life, and in their career, because we had honest conversations about their most natural way to influence. Working with people and understanding who they are and what their strengths are helps us to both understand where they can best influence the world. That is powerful. That helps them understand who they are. That helps them find significance in their careers and life. That helps them influence in a way that is more powerful than they could ever imagine.

Appreciate and seize the opportunity you have to help others. There is nothing so rewarding. While my career has brought me many accolades and financial success- there is nothing more rewarding to me than when an employee that I have mentored or coached comes up to me years later and tells me that I made a difference in their lives and careers and goes on to share a memory of a time in the past when my influence has impacted them. That is Gold. That reminds that "I am what I am" and to savor it.

MAVERICK ACTION

FOUR KEY WORDS THAT DEFINE ACTIONS WITH CLARITY

Purpose

Goal

Action

Result

This Maverick action is truly one of my catalyst. I created it because when I was in the corporate world I consistently found myself in meeting after meeting feeling like time was being wasted and often feeling like we didn't know what we were meeting for. Have you ever experienced that? You come out of an executive meeting only to feel that you've accomplished nothing. If we take an action and don't clearly understand the purpose for taking it, it can leave us feeling shallow and void, and lacking substance.

This Maverick action became universal once I started to see its true value in so many other ways.

Let me share an example with you. Let's say you are launching a website, start this project by writing down these four words on a piece of paper: **Purpose**, **Goal**, **Action**, and **Result.** Then ask yourself "what is the purpose for this website?", "what is the goal I have set for this website?", "what are the actions I need to take to develop it?", "what are the results when I do?".

Let's say that the only purpose for your new website is to educate others about your products or services, it's not a revenue generator for you at this point in business. Once you understand that it's an educational platform you'll focus your content and actions on bringing those things forward, rather than focusing on adding a shopping cart, sharing your rates or the many other things that go along with a website designed as an income generator.

You can see by clarifying the purpose of your website it allows you to align goals, take actions and ultimately, you'll receive the results you've set out for it. This allows you to manage your expectations for this project and better understand the return-on-investment.

With clear purpose, we understand how we must move forward or the reason we're even doing it in the first place.

The next step is setting the goal. Without clear goals we don't know what to strive for. For this particular example, two goals could be to establish name recognition and credibility within the marketplace. You're not looking to monetize the website itself, rather gain business just by the credibility and presence it gives you. It shows that you're a professional. These goals make it easier to define what should be included in your actions to ensure you get the results that you've set out to receive.

Now let's take actions. The actions to accomplish your goals are to create a user-friendly website that profiles what you do and the value you bring, this establishes the credibility you desire. A second action would be to spread the word and drive traffic to your site. This can be done by handing out business cards at professional events, utilizing social media networking, and creating quality content that people will visit your site to see.

With this strategic system of establishing then working off of purpose, goals and actions, the results are much easier to plan for and obtain. It turns a ledge into stairs, a visible and workable route for you to follow.

This is a great exercise to have others on your team take too. If you find that one of your junior partners or rookie sales team members consistently takes actions that are not producing results or taking on projects that are not making a difference, invite them to write down these four words, show them how to take the time to really ask themselves more about what they are doing. Have them clearly define the purpose for doing it and set clear goals toward achieving what they'd like to see from the time they put towards it. Now they can see what kind of laser focus this gives the actions they take. No longer wasting time, or feeling frustrated or lost.

Don't just stop at purpose though, go deep and dig into the goals, the actions and the results too. You now have a sage strategy that you can take that's quite easy and gives you what you want without a lot of overthinking or stressing. Just understanding and doing.

MAVERICK ACTION

WRITE AN ESSAY ON 'WHAT MONEY MEANS TO YOU'

Money is at the root level for all of us. No one is immune to wanting more of it. The value we place on money is a different thing however.

A bold Maverick action to take is to sit with your thoughts on money, then write down what it means to you and why you desire more of it. This action will assist you in removing blocks or barriers you have with money. It's starts with *how you think* about money. Getting specific is important.

Questions to assist you;

» What *beliefs* do you have that *are engrained* in how you think about money?

» Why do you desire more money?

» Is making money tied to your worth? If so, why?

» Are you a good steward of your money? If so, why?

» What will you do with access money (invest or spend)?

  » Go deeper into why you'd do either or both

» How much does confidence feed into your ability to make more money?

» Do you have a 'lack-of' mindset around money? If so, why?

» For you to feel that you have enough money, what is the exact amount you need? How do you arrive at that number? Why?

» Other thoughts around money...

Once you flush your thinking out, now write an essay. It can be a sentence, paragraph or page on "what money means to you". This becomes your guiding force and personal roadmap to obtaining more.

MAGNETISM AND MONEY

I like to say 'passion not paychecks' for a reason. I know that when I stay in the passion zone of obtaining clients, creating projects and serving others, the money naturally 'shows up'. Yes, I did just say 'show up'. From my experience with money, when you perform you get paid. You will also be paid your worth. That's my entire brand focus, assisting you in understanding how your value, talents, self-worth and self-esteem align so you don't have to chase money or the many other areas of success you desire, rather, you learn that you can attract it, this is where money starts to align to your value and worth overall. With this level of purity and integrity around money, it instantly removes blocks and barriers and opens you up to receiving more, in multiple areas in both business and in life.

I choose to stay in the passion zone, this allows me to operate at a level of peace and ease which attracts more peace and ease and when it feels peaceful and easy, it no longer resists me. It attracts more of the right types of people that will pay the money for the service and offerings I provide.

How Does This Make You Feel About Money?

When we're in conflict in any area of our life, it rages war on us. I choose to say grounded in my desires, which allows me to operate at a level of purity and ease. That matters to me. It's genuine and it's one of the many reasons why I chose to develop my own personal brand. You don't have to agree with my approach, methodology or mindset around money and achievement, but it's worked for me and many others, so I invite you in to these ideas of ease. Give them a try and see if you operate differently. If you like the shift, implement it for yourself. That's a gift I give to you. You deserve to feel good about what you do and how you earn. You have value. I know this. You know this. Go for more in a way that serves you.

Maverick Characteristics:

Action & Performance

"Actions are the fundamentals of performance and achievement."

Watch Maverick Video FIVE:

High Performance

Watch Maverick Video SIX:

It's time to ask yourself, what are you afraid of?

The videos that accompany these Maverick mantras can be found on my YouTube playlist The Making of a Maverick

Wow! Performance lights me up! This is the topic that I could talk late into the night about. I always knew that if I performed well it would pay off. It's this high-performance mindset that's allowed me great achievements.

The words "Action" and "Performance" are often interchangeable. However, there's a distinction you should know; actions are motions to be completed, but performance requires intention. Without passion, clarity, and vision, we are unable to perform. Sure, we might check a few tasks off a list but without intention it won't feel right. This happens when we do the right things over and over again - performance is the long game and I'm here to tell you that without that long-distance vision, you won't move forward.

I don't have a traditional college degree (by choice). My education is comprised of experience, networking, and personal research. I've learned by doing and have let my experience guide me and by watching and researching others. One of the main things I've learned about performance is this; actions can and will show you your value. I always say "when you perform, you get paid." enough said.

Performance was and always has been my paycheck. I've never taken a salaried position, I've always felt that salaries cap your potential (my opinion). Instead of being told what I'm worth, I'd rather perform and see what happens. This goes with my risk-taking mindset and fearlessness. When you're a commission-based professional or an independent in business you have unlimited potential and opportunity, I've always enjoyed these roles and the challenges that come with them. You're given the ability to write your own paycheck every month. But it must be matched to desire, intentions and actions. You can't just think about the number, you've got to take actions to receive it.

I find challenge and opportunity lies heavily with our performance. That's exciting for champions and Mavericks, and those who choose to empower themselves to get ahead. I believe this is where the term 'skies the limit' comes from. There is no cap to how far you can go. It becomes more of what you desire and crafting a plan to get there. You can't have this level of high-performance-desire without a good plan or systems though. Doing so is like shooting an arrow with no target or bullseye, there's no real way to measure it. Wishing to be a good performer or a high achiever makes no sense, but having a good plan will get you there. By implementing systems it's much easier to execute a plan and arrive at your goals.

Here's an example of a way to implement a system to utilize right away:

Let's say you need a strong intake system to onboard your clients or new team members to your company when they join you. Wouldn't it be helpful to have a system in place when someone says "yes, I'm joining you", you can say "great, I'll send you the necessary forms, documents and intake process to get you started". Now, turn to that system that you've created to onboard your new team member and let it go to work for you. You'll have the process nailed down, all the correspondence that goes with it and by doing so, gives you back time because it's already created and all you have to do is execute from these systems.

As I've previously stated; "dreams not written down are simply wishes". This goes for goals too. If you don't write down the goals that you've set and chart a solid plan to get there, you'll forever be chasing them. Rather, approach it with power and clarity and state what you desire, utilize the Maverick mantra we've shared with you to; **"Speak What You Want To See"**, then create the plan to get there. Now you are empowered by your choices and can focus on allowing and trusting that you've created the right plan of action to get you there. The cool part here is that implementation of systems also allows you to implement safety nets. What I mean by this is, you can make it part of your system to stop, recalibrate, test, and measure. Instead of completely failing at a task, frequent recalibration allows you to make small adjustments and pivot which gets you to your goal faster. Try something new, but implement and utilize this safety net to ensure that your mistakes do not become your habits.

CLARITY = HIGH PERFORMANCE

Having clarity of the goals you'd like to achieve gives you the first steps to high performance.

It's one thing to be a high performer, but it also has to be matched to systems to ensure sustainability. Without the ability to sustain your performance it will easily start to overwhelm you. You'll become tired and drained and start to underperform because you simply can't keep up with the demand.

Systems feed sustainability, it's these systems that allow for greater performance. You don't have to rework the wheel when you have systems. Create them, tweak them, revisit them often, omit the systems that don't work, and enhance the ones that do. It's within the system structure that makes high performance happen.

CREATING BOUNDARIES

Creating a system allows you more predictable openings in your schedules where boundaries can be placed to keep you balanced. This is so important when it comes to long-term goals, especially businesses that have small teams or a singular person running the brand.

In my coaching practice, I serve my clients on certain days of the week and at certain times. This allows me to achieve the goals I've set while leaving plenty of room for growth, but also matching it to a high-performance coaching calendar. Without the clarity of first understanding what I'd like to see happen I wouldn't know how many clients I needed to coach each week or how many hours I needed for self-care and family obligations. When considering your goals, it's also important to consider how much time you want to spend outside of your business or profession. If I didn't have a systematic approach to all aspects of life, I'd enter into every week haphazardly. When everyone and everything else starts to take over your health, focus, and performance it's time to recalibrate and implement systems. It becomes their schedule and their timing and not yours, if you keep that up long enough, eventually, you'll become very snarky giving away all of that personal time by allowing them the power to control it for you. It becomes more about choice. When you choose it, you become empowered. When you're told how to do it, and on what terms, that can make us dissatisfied and powerless.

Don't put systems in place just to say you've got systems. Get clear on what you need systems for then maximize them to death. Systems, performance, healthy boundaries, and safety nets...these should light you up and give you fuel to perform at your highest levels.

MAVERICK MANTRA

"SYSTEMS = PERFORMANCE"

There are three key components to high performance, they are; being **active** and **consistent** and **recalibrating** (which means to test and measure to ensure you're getting results).

Simply put; creating clear actions then consistently taking those actions allows you to perform.

Stepped out, it looks like this;

» First, define what performance means to you.

Performance is defined as what goals, outcomes or achievements you're striving for:

Then define what **actions** you need to take to arrive at those goals, outcomes and achievements:

Now, create the **systems** necessary to execute on.

Now, **consistently** take those actions.

Now, stop every three months, twelve weeks, or 90 days (each quarter) to reflect back a.k.a. **recalibrate**, to the actions you've taken to see what's worked for you.

This recalibration exercise shows you immediately what you can remove or add to your systems to ensure success and move forward into Maverick status.

I've discovered that there is one main component that gets dropped easily. I've seen this so many times that I've developed a strategy to assist in getting through it (see the Maverick action below);

Which one of these do you think gets dropped the easiest?

» Taking **actions**
» **Consistency** taking the actions
» **Recalibrating** and revisiting the actions

If you guessed, consistency, you're right! It's not what actions to take and defining with clarity what those are, but it's *our consistent behavior* of taking the actions that gets dropped first. Recalibrating is easy because you really only have to do this, four times a year or every quarter, 12 weeks, 90 days take a quick reflection back to what you've done and what you've achieved.

It's that crazy consistency component that keeps us stuck or is the reason we fall off-track.

Look at weight loss as the example here; we are all very aware of the actions to take, eat right, exercise, drink water, those are clear. What can get hard after a while is consistently eating right and/or exercising. For whatever reason, we may choose to drop consistently taking an action we know works, we understand the value it brings and the reason for doing it but we either get bored, or even overconfident, thinking that we know how to do it but how easily these old habits or behaviors can creep back in making us gain some or all of the weight back. I've done this a few times, I've been a serial weight loss champion over the years. I know what it feels like to make the decision to either stop exercising or stop eating healthy and gain weight back only to get back at it and engrain the healthy habits to keep at it for the long haul.

Maverick Action: To overcome that consistency component, here's what you can do. **Write an essay on the word consistency**. Just like I encouraged you to do with the money essay; it can be a sentence, paragraph or page, but get clear on what consistency means to you. It's when you clearly understand how it serves you and why you should consistently take actions, or the understanding of what stops you from doing it, then you'll be able to implement this for the long haul, becoming a high performer, champion or Maverick.

MAVERICK MANTRA

"IF YOU EDUCATE PROPERLY, THE SALE AUTOMATICALLY HAPPENS"

Watch Maverick Video SEVEN:

If You Educate Properly, the Sale Automatically Happens

The video that accompanies this Maverick mantra can be found on my YouTube playlist The Making of a Maverick

I was working with a client, and he told me that his business was growing, but the process of selling didn't feel right. He was passionate about his company and the products they offered, but it didn't feel good when sealing the deal. He wasn't closing business and could sense internally that he was pressuring his prospects instead of taking a genuine approach and aligning to new clients with integrity. He had to make a shift in his thinking and how he approached his offering. I shared this Maverick mantra with him and it changed everything. This client secured $75,000 in business in less than 72 hours with this mantra. It works, here's how;

Educate Properly and the Sale Will Happen.

When I say educate, I mean more than mentioning how a product or service works and what it does. Focus the discussion on how it helps them, share the value other clients have received by using it, or owning one, and why you're so excited to represent it. This excitement is contagious, and will shift that final question from "will you?" to "why WOULDN'T you?".

It's easy to fall back into a pitch when you're nervous about a potential sale, so here are my top three tips to help shift your thinking:

Make a List

Start by listing five things that you LOVE about what you do or what you offer, then refer to those when meeting with your prospect. This immediately removes all the 'sales lingo' and takes you straight to the pure intention of why it's so powerful that they utilize this product, service or offering.

It's easy for you to share in these terms too. It's a lot less about making the sale and becomes more about connecting to the value and why it's so dang important to have it or implement it or own it.

When I was selling handbags, I loved sharing some key components about the handbag itself. It was natural for this to ooze out of me and I often times couldn't stop talking about all the assets and features. Doing this wasn't about the sale, it was all about how fun and easy carrying this handbag would be. It immediately shifted what I shared about the actual product, immediately removing the pressure to sell, and rather moved me into a space of clear purpose for the product. They were fabric handbags, so the ease of carrying something so light and all those fabric options was often times where I would start. Diving right into why it was so easy to carry one naturally aligned the sale to happen because if anything, my sheer enthusiasm for it won them over every time. Then the question became "how many would you like to take home with you", and the sales increased so naturally that it was fun to just show up and talk about why these were the best products on the market that everyone just had to have one.

When you educate and share features, benefits, and personal loves that you have with the product, service or offering, others immediately align to this and can't help but say yes to it. Again, you're *not selling, just sharing*, and this removes the pressure.

I reference the sale of handbags, but this can apply to most any product you're selling, whether it be selling a home with its jacuzzi tub and walk-in closet, or you're a car dealer and you've chosen this specific line of cars because you believe so passionately about their reliability. It's about how you educate and represent why you've chosen to sell that product or service that gets others to trust and purchase from you.

STOP AND LISTEN

Have you ever considered recording yourself making the sale? Take the time to record your positioning of your offer and how you educate your prospects, you'll immediately sense your tone. You'll hear if you sound desperate for the sale, or are you lighting up so brilliantly that you've got them so dang excited that they just have to have what you're offering. Your voice inflection can tell you a lot.

Do you feel constricted and hear yourself trying so hard to make the sale that you might as well just come out and say "look, are you going to buy one or what?" or do you have that peace and ease about you in how you're talking about it and sharing it?

Is your voice coming out in a way that attracts the yes? Or are you listening to fingers on the chalkboard trying to make the sale happen? Only when you listen back will you be able to connect to the vibe you're putting off and how you're communicating about it that aligns the sale.

Sales is all about trust. Do you sound like a trusting person? Someone who you should buy the product from, someone who you should obtain the service from? You have it within you, but how are you releasing it? A few simple tweaks to your approach could change everything. Are you sharing the most important features about what you have? Are you talking too much that you drown the person who's trying to listen and learn about the product from you? If so, stop and ask a few key questions like, "if you could learn three things about this product or service in the next five minutes, what would they be?" Bam! Now, they are serving you what you need to learn on a silver platter just by switching things up a bit and asking them a few questions.

This is where you are educating yourself for the sale. Not assuming that you are going to share all they want or need to learn before they can say yes, but more of a collaborative partnership and synergy to it.

RECALIBRATE AND REACH OUT!

If you have identified issues that would make you not want to buy from you, change it! Reach out to others on your team or successful professionals in your field that are doing things the way you want to do them and ask for help. Work with a coach or mentor to identify what you can enhance or share that will get you a "YES" every time.

A week later, my client shared how excited he was with this new approach. It was much easier and less stressful during his prospect meetings. He happily reported that adjusting his approach allowed him to successfully close business in a way that "just felt right." To me, when business feels right, that's a success. And isn't that what this is all about?

I challenge you to shift your focus from selling to educating and sharing, then reflecting on what it has done for your business goals. Make a list of five things that you love getting out of bed and offering to others that you know makes a difference, then get out there and speak it! "The ask" is inevitable. However, when we transform a sale from a transaction to a conversation, we allow room for more authenticity and an opportunity for business to feel right.

MAVERICK CASE STUDY

ALISON TURNER, SALES LEADER

Alison and I came together many moons ago, during one of my first leadership roles and the fact that we are still connected and in touch today says something.

I've told Alison this a thousand times, but if I were to look in the mirror and it were to reflect back someone who most mirrors both my mindset and my actions, I'd have to say Alison!

She's one of those catalyst people in my life that I've had the privilege to work with, and get to know on a personal level. We became fast friends as we both led high-level teams together. I've learned a lot from her and I am grateful we share such commonalities between us.

What I enjoy the most about Alison has been her hard work and determination. She's not one to ever give up and knows how to put her all into what she does. Her performance is proven, it's led to her success. She is someone who understands the power of performance and how our abilities feed into it.

As the leader I've witnessed in Alison, she knows the value of people, systems, hard work, performance and many other attributes to being a champion and Maverick. We joke about it not being easy, but fun. She lights up at the challenge of striving and enjoying what she does, it's kept her in the independent arena as she's gone on to lead large and wildly successful teams on a nationwide level. She's done it for multiple companies, which proves that she knows what she is doing.

I'm grateful to know Alison and call her a friend, and had to include her in our book. She is a true, pure Maverick.

Let her story of action and performance feed you. She serves others at a high level and knows their value. I appreciate this. It's easy for me to align to her thinking and follow what Alison does.

This is what Alison shares;

When I look back at my story as an entrepreneur it begins years ago as a 10-year-old girl, pulling her red wagon around the neighborhood with my dad's fresh garden produce, selling door to door. I remember this experience vividly, approaching a house, asking them "Would you like to buy some vegetables?" I would proudly go home with my $5-10 in my pocket. Those earnings were HUGE back then. I can remember just doing it, not really thinking about it, asking and no matter what the answer, going to the next door.

Fast forward to 1991, I graduated from high school and headed to the big city. Growing up in a small Midwestern town was amazing, I would never change it, that will always be home but heading off to a city school with the world in front of me, was my goal and dream. I wanted to see the world, meet people from everywhere, experience city living. I graduated with a Bachelor in Social Work from Augsburg College in Minnesota in 1995. My experience there was one of growth, challenge, real life learning and my start to becoming a strong independent woman.

I spent 4 years in the Social Work field and enjoyed it immensely, helping others, caring for and empowering women mainly in the Domestic Violence and Women's Issues arenas. During this time, being a young working professional, it was challenging and rewarding as the field can be, it did not meet my goals for myself of becoming financially independent and being able to show and grow into becoming a strong leader. I knew there was not a lot of room to be me and I wanted more.

My career then took a turn to the business arena. I spent 7 years in retail management where I ran retails stores of $3 million and plus a year in revenue. This is where I began to flourish. I earned the president's club award (top 10% of sales managers) 3 years in a row with a retailer of over 1,000 stores. This is when I realized I was excited and challenge by recognition and rewards. My fire was lit and I wanted more.

Onto the business/corporate world I went to run a team and company as a Sales Leader and Team Manager. I spent 6 years in this field and worked for a small employer in which during that time, I gained Human Resources training and knowledge, management skills of teams and sales leadership in an organization of both employees and independents. A move out of state brought this role to an end.

In 2006, my husband's job took us to Oregon. He accepted a promotion that we could not pass up. We moved to Oregon where I knew no one. We had two small children at the time, where expecting our 3rd. Knowing that motherhood was my #1 priority, I embraced that role and realized that "working", "going for it" would have to wait. During my mothering and pregnancy, I stumbled on a small, startup business in Iowa through a friend. It turned out to be my gift. I saw women having fun, loving a fun product and I thought.... I can do that. It would get me out of the house, be my girl time, my socializing time, make new friends time and I was in desperate need of finding me.

I was the first representative in the state of Oregon, I earned top sales honors, top team building honors and a free incentive trip along with what I call "getting a degree in business." It was a wonderful time in my life as I raised my babies, found myself and started to dream again of all the possibilities that life had in store for me!

My story continues, this is the part of being a maverick...going for it, it's not and was not always easy, but worth it.

My husband and I now had 3 wonderful kiddos, Sydney was 6, Reese was 4 and Carson was 1. My husband was with a Billion-dollar company and had been there for 19 years when one day in May, they are laying off and let him know he is no longer needed. Wow, what a blow. We are now wondering what do we do, where do we go! Gratefully we stayed strong, a team, a family through amazing challenge as my husband found a new job 6 months later.

This time was one of small children, sleepless nights, stress, my husband feeling lost at times, our marriage strained not only financially but emotionally... We knew if we were going to get through it, it would be because we chose too. So, we chose to, we planned and took date night once a week (no matter the cost, definitely cheaper than divorce) we prayed, we loved, we continued to work to better our family and in the end, our journey took us to Madison, Wisconsin for a new position for my husband. During this move, the sales organization that I had been aligned with for 5 years was no longer going to be in business, the changing economy had hit and they could no longer sustain. I had a new road to find and found it with Lia Sophia. I had met an amazing friend, someone I admire who was in the business and I knew in my heart, that my path was calling me to continue to run my own race, make my own hours and achieve my goals. I knew Lia Sophia could be this for me. My kids were still little and I needed the flexibility to be mom first. I began my journey of 4 1/2 years with an amazing company! My husband was settled and my business was growing.

During my time with Lia Sophia, I earned many honors and awards .... top 10 in personal sales, 4 incentive trips for my husband and I, top recruiting honors and more. My biggest most prized accomplishment was the growth I was showing in my business each year, I could see this being a long-term journey.

We know nothing is guaranteed and in December of 2014, I was again reminded of this as Lia Sophia announced they were closing. How could this be as I was at the top of my game and my "business" was running, succeeding, thriving?

I began my 'year of strong' I call it. 2015 brought so much good now that I look back...discovery, failure, going back to "work", digging deep, digging deeper to not doubt me, I know me, I can be anything I want to be and by December of 2015, I found my next door. LuLaRoe came to me through a peer friend of mine and I remember calling her and saying let's do this...I thought for a minute, again, build again, start over, but that lasted a minute as I knew I have done it before, I can and I will do it again.

I've grown my personal boutique business to over $250,000+ in revenue and my team across the country is over $2 million+ and growing. I get to own my own fashion boutique, run my business, work on my terms, have the flexibility and freedom to manage and love on my family all while going for it. Dreaming big, taking my one chance at life and making it count. Empowering women on my team to dream bigger, achieve more...helping my customers feel beautiful putting their best foot forward in life that is what I get to spend my days doing and I would not have it any other way.

Every step of my life and specifically the last 10 years has led me to today and I am grateful. I know nothing is guaranteed but with hard work, leadership, confidence, passion and love for what I do, anything is possible, today and always.

MAVERICK CASE STUDY

CARISSA KRUSE, FOUNDER, WEDDINGS BY CARUE

Carissa was building out a nationwide brand with a product and service she had created but was tapping out and only getting so far because that is where the vision for her business stopped. Carissa was only picturing what was happening during the 4-year timespan of working her business before we met. When we met and started working together to bust through this cycle she had created, everything began to shift. It was easy for me to run next to her as she clarified her vision and I challenged her to think bigger. So big, that within the first year of us working together her business grew by 650%. Numbers don't lie, and this was substantial growth.

The plan was enhanced, the actions were bigger, the team and all the details started to align and it was happening. Carissa was witnessing her dream and desire to build a nationwide brand. The cool part was how humble she stayed throughout the entire process. It was always a delight working with her because we spent most of our time giggling through it all. As I continued to compound strategies to work on and implement, she became so tuned-in with the challenge, that it was fun and easy.

Now, sustainability was next. The only way to ensure achievement is to also implement sustainability. Because without a consistent level of execution and recalibrating it's easy to fall off course or to lose which direction comes next. So, we continued to map out the vision together and during the next 12 months her business did what she said it was going to do; it became a nationwide brand. She was empowering all kinds of people throughout the U.S. to sell and represent her products and services, clearly putting her on the map and exceeding goals.

Without Carissa coming and being open to receive coaching, and learning how to "**speak what she wanted to see**", would any of this have happened. Carissa is a Maverick and her story needs to be told to inspire you to keep going and to dream bigger than you ever thought possible. You hear these words, but below Carissa shares her personal experience.

This is what Carissa shares on her terms, nothing written below here has been changed:

I had so many ideas and goals for Weddings by Carue. When I first met with Marlo, she helped me navigate through these ideas by incorporating fundamental processes and strategies along the way which has led to growth and results. Marlo has this way of inspiring you to stretch yourself. One of her signature motivational tactics are bright star sticky notes. She wrote a sticky note one time that says: "What do I need the most right now?" I still have this sticky note in my notebook and ask myself this question as I continue to build the business.

What did I learn from my time with Marlo? I can tell you everything I learned was invaluable. She has provided so many ideas, strategies and connections that I continue to pull from daily.

I created Weddings by Carue to help people, help people do what they love and help couples have a wedding of their dreams whether through invitations, photography, photo booths, or cinematography. Creating a business that is based around how we can help others is so rewarding. When I set out in building this business model it was a challenge as we offer service based products as well as tangible products. Each product has different marketing strategies.

When building a business, you need to dig in and figure out what does your client want? View it from your clients' eyes. Providing something that your client wants draws your clients to you and makes them feel connected with you and your product and brand.

Building a business takes a good idea, hard work, dedication and strategy. Strategy is the most important piece when building and expanding the business. I learned that strategy is not just about the numbers, it is about creating plans and building connections that you can bounce ideas off of. Creating your "tribe" as Marlo calls it. Who is your tribe? Who can you call to talk about your business strategies with?

One of my favorite parts about building a business is being creative, the options are endless. There is no right or wrong, but you can know you are headed in the right direction through analyzation, research and strategy. Strategy has really helped Weddings by Carue get to the next level much quicker and allowed us to think through many possible options.

As we expanded the invitation line nationwide we looked at several sales platforms and worked through the different options. Strategy was key when building the direct sales platform as it had to be unique, sellable and different. Strategy helped us create our own unique hybrid sales model. We wanted a platform that would provide people an opportunity to enhance their client offerings, experience and make money selling truly custom invitations without the backend work. With Weddings by Carue taking care of the graphic design, printing and shipping, anyone can join the Weddings by Carue team and sell invitations. Our model is made for current businesses (ex: event planners, venues, florists) to add or enhance an invitation line as well as anyone interested in becoming a direct sales representative part time or full time. With our exclusive sales process and kit, invitations can be sold in as little as 15 minutes. We wanted our vendor partners to have an opportunity to add invitations, but from our analysis and feedback from vendors they do not have a lot of time to spend with clients, so a quick and easy process was required.

Building a business is not easy and having someone that can give you that encouragement, extra nudge and strategize with, helps to motivate and keep you headed in the right direction.

Now it is your turn to build and grow that business or idea that you have burning inside you! Think strategic, be strategic and your results and growth will follow.

MAVERICK ACTION

CLOSING THE SUCCESS GAP

When my clients decide to hire me as a coach, I come in with the expectation that they have a goal they want to meet. It's my job to assess the situation and get a better understanding of where my client is in the process of meeting his or her goals. In order to get an idea of where they are mentally in pursuit of their goal I ask a question with a quantifiable answer. I ask them how big of a gap is sitting between them and their definition of success, in a percentage.

One client responded with a 60% gap. It seemed strange to me, because I could only see a 16% gap between her and her goals. This outside vantage point is a key element of coaching. An expert can read people and can see the potential, even when it seems hidden from oneself. Having a coach gives you an unbiased opinion that often puts things into perspective. My client was shocked that I could only see a 16% gap based on her answers to my questions. I pointed out the value pieces and once she viewed herself in a larger context, she was able to see how close she really was to her goals.

So, how did we approach closing her success gap?

I continued to listen to the goals she had set for herself and her company, then I assisted in creating a plan composed of business strategies that have been proven to be successful. Week over week, she took actions that moved her into the right direction and things started taking off for her. Despite the fact that there was a 44% difference between where she thought and where I thought she was in relation to her goal – she took the actions we discussed and gained the success she was striving for.

Through our strategic motivational jam sessions around the success gap issue, I'm happy to report that this client successfully implemented the necessary strategies to meet her goals to grow and close more businesses overall.

MAVERICK ACTION

RECORD YOURSELF DURING A BUSINESS HIGH

Have you ever told yourself "I've hit a slump and don't know exactly how to get out of it"?

You've got to take a proactive approach to your success. I've found that one of the greatest actions you can take toward avoiding the 'slump' is to prepare yourself that someday it's going to come, this Maverick action will assist in being ready when it arrives. It will. It happens to all of us.

Record yourself during a 'career high point', yep, that simple! *Record yourself speaking your success.* What you did, how you did it, the formula or strategies you used, the people or processes you aligned with. Put it to words then LISTEN to your own excitement and energy when you were 'hitting it out of the ballpark' or achieving some level of success in your career or business.

It doesn't take long, maybe 10 minutes. I recommend downloading AudioNote.

It's amazing how powerful it can be when you're just not feeling it or no longer in the game, how listening to your own optimism, momentum and success can quickly pick you up and remind yourself that you've done it before so you have it in you to do it again.

Give it a try, it's simple and cost-effective and the results are priceless! Performance is a beautiful thing. You deserve to get out of the slump and back into the game.

MAVERICK CHARACTERISTIC

CONFIDENCE

"Leverage weekly wins to get bigger results"

Watch Maverick Video EIGHT:
Confidence

The video that accompanies this Maverick characteristic can be found on my YouTube playlist The Making of a Maverick

What is it about confidence that allows us to take risk? Did you know that it may be your lack of confidence that's keeping you from taking bigger actions and risks and stretching outside of your comfort zone?

Personally, my worth is not valued in money, it is rooted in peace-of-mind. It's my desire to relentlessly pursue my passions never chasing a paycheck. When I have peace and ease and I feel completely grounded in who I am and the actions I'm taking, that fuels my self-worth. I feel that once we define and tap into our worth in life through our actions, purpose, and execution we have immediately tapped into our self-esteem. It's about how we show up in the world and not how others perceive us. Knowing your self-worth means having unlimited confidence to ask for the sale, ask for the salary you desire, ask for the project to oversee, ask to take the lead, to take bigger actions which will produce bigger results.

Stand in conviction and face your fears. Know your value and bring it into the world in a vast and powerful way that inspires others to be bigger as well. We all lead by example with the actions we take. We are constantly being watched by our kids, our families, our friends, our co-workers, and our communities. Start to lead yourself in a way that others want to follow.

MAVERICK MANTRA

"EVERYONE WANTS WHAT I HAVE TO OFFER"

Watch Maverick Video NINE:
Everyone Wants What I Have to Offer

The video that accompanies this Maverick mantra can be found on
my YouTube playlist The Making of a Maverick

The return that this particular mantra brings is powerful. When I found myself speaking this mantra **"everyone wants what I have to offer,"** things immediately became easier. A huge shift in my power and thinking toward closing business changed and deals started closing. Why? Because how we talk to ourselves is where it all begins. It's highly unlikely that anyone is telling you you're not enough, or your product.. or offering is not enough. You are stopping your success by having a mindset focused on what you believe you are lacking.

ATTRACT VS. PURSUE

The only way to attract and not pursue is to have the confidence to speak to yourself so powerfully that it gets others aligned to that power. When you're confident, you attract more confidence. It's easier for people to start trusting you, because you trust in yourself. It's easy to keep those naysayers an arm's length away when you can trust yourself at this root level and have the ability to speak **'everyone wants what I have to offer'**. Go into a client meeting or your annual performance review and share what you're doing, but share it in a way that gets others believing in it too.

When you set yourself up with a high level of conviction and belief, it's easier for others to attract to it. If you're thinking it, others are hearing it and seeing it and you don't even have to say a thing. It's oozing out of you. So, if you come into the room and ask for the sale with a mindset focused on what you lack, others can already sense that you're questioning yourself which keeps them from buying it, believing it or wanting it.

SHIFT YOUR MINDSET

On the drive to your next client meeting or as you enter into your weekly networking event, tell yourself **'everyone wants what I have to offer'**. This is all about checking the ego at the door, and fueling yourself up with your own personal power. Use this Maverick mantra and you'll win every time.

Here's a breakdown of confidence vs competition and why you'd want to implement attraction rather than pursuit.

Attract = Confidence

Pursue = Compete

When We Attract:

» We have a gentle hum.

» We're more efficient.

» We have higher levels of performance.

» We understand our values, talents and self-worth.

» We focus on the right types of actions.

» We spend time improving ourselves, not worrying about others' actions.

When We Pursue:

» Pursuit kills confidence.

» We have a 'lack of' mindset.

» We chase, not stand in conviction and attract.

   » We feel like we have to be more, feel that we're not enough.

» We think we'll never be at that level.

» We don't think we can make things happen.

» We put off a 'static, edgy vibe' (let's be honest, we're negative).

PUTTING IT TO WORK

During my podcast interview with Mark Brodinsky, (you can listen to that interview on my podcast 22 Motivational Minutes with Marlo found on my website www.marlohiggins.com) he asked, "Marlo, what is it about you that thinks you can build Mavericks and champions?" My response is easy. It's as easy as painting a picture so clear that the person only sees themselves achieving it.

We start with defining the ultimate goal or outcome. Then clearly paint that picture. Never worrying about the 'how', that comes naturally, but the clarity of the vision and the end result in what you are striving for is all that matters right now.

In my interview, we use the analogy of a thoroughbred running the race at the Kentucky Derby. I describe how the jockey gets that horse to run full on fast and achieve that goal of winning. Reaching the finish line because it is well conditioned, prepared and has the mindset, while in the shoot that they are the winner. The one to take home the blue ribbon. When you can feel it, and see it with that level of depth, you achieve it. The thoroughbred I mention has been trained to know that they are the winner. They are ready to run their race. They see what it takes to cross the finish line. They are 'jockeyed up' and ready. The jockey knows they will win. Together, they do because all they can vision is crossing the finish line and being awarded the trophy.

Strength gives us power. In order to have high levels of mental strength, we have to do what it takes to understand deep down what our self-worth/self-esteem truly is. What is it about us, what do we possess that really makes a difference? What is that power for you?

What happens is, you become fully empowered. When you have a high and healthy level of self-worth and self-esteem you can do anything. It naturally removes any obstacles or barriers and fear because you start to rely on your inner power, you are now fully empowered to achieve. You stop thinking and start doing. You have strength in your ability, in your vision, in your preparation, in all that you do.

MAVERICK MANTRA

"YOU CAN'T APOLOGIZE, AND YOU CAN'T MAKE EXCUSES"

Watch Maverick Video TEN:

You Can't Apologize, and You Can't Make Excuses

The video that accompanies this Maverick mantra can be found on my YouTube playlist The Making of a Maverick

Within our brand, we have this rule that you can't apologize and you can't make excuses. Why do we even have such a rule? Too many times, folks come to the table with "I'm sorry, I'm sorry, I'm sorry" or a laundry list of excuses that are keeping them stuck. When you're a champion or a Maverick this type of behavior becomes disempowering and weak. It became clear we needed to adopt these rules with the clients we serve and how we serve them for them to understand and believe their worth. Remember, we share that self-worth is tied directly to our self-esteem.

This mantra has helped me personally through times when I was ready to throw in the towel and just give up. But the easy reminder of 'no excuses, no apologies', resonated so deeply that if I did find myself with this type of mindset, I was better equipped to tap into my "why" and have the strength to forge ahead and not give up on myself or the project.

As I was writing this book, I experienced another setback out of the blue with being at the 82% completion point. I remember coming home from my upcoming surgery appointment and telling my husband that I should just give all of this up and focus on getting myself better and allow myself to heal and remove the pressure of submitting the manuscript and just scrapping the entire project, one that I had put so much focus to and had rallied others around. He looked at me and said, "That's not you. You never give up no matter how hard things get. You're just in a low place right now, you don't really mean that."

I needed that outside reminder that I don't give up. I reminded myself that I was nearly finished and it was worth seeing it to the finish line, even if it meant pushing back the date to submit the manuscript to the team.

And if I did not walk this talk myself and have a healthy self-belief, I'm pretty certain that day I would have just thrown in the towel. I was at a point of complete defeat. I was looking at yet another setback as a sign to give up. It was a combination of my support system and my own strategies that pulled me from that place of defeat and reminded me that I had a purpose to serve, sharing these mantras and strategies with each of you.

I'd come too far, I'm too rooted in my value and my worth and my understanding that this is yet another reason why I'm aligned to be the one to share the message of this book. I'm here to inspire and show you that you're worth it. You matter. All those hard things that come, or when we're being challenged and tested, if we are truly meant to bring it forward, we'll keep going. We'll allow and let them come, knowing that these struggles are serving us, making us stronger, giving us greater wisdom, and power.

So, I accepted my own grit, and stopped the excuses, and I didn't allow myself to apologize to myself for even wanting to throw in the towel. Instead, I took my husband's advice and kept at it. I know that I've been called on to bring this body of work into the world to serve others. This is the reason why I can easily tell you that these mantras are not one of a boastful spirit, but rather a badass kick in the pants to do it. Allow it. Go for it. Make it happen. Be a Maverick, strive for champion status. Get off the bench, get into the game and show up to go up.

Stop making excuses and apologizing. Those things will never work for you. *Doing* and *being* will.

I'll also share that because my mindset tanked and I allowed it to feed me negatively, I also allowed myself to feed myself more, gaining weight and giving up on my healthy status. Allowing excuses to creep into the performance of my health. I stopped walking daily and started eating more crap, because I was giving up on myself. I was no longer interested in being that healthy, vivacious person that I'd worked so hard to achieve at being.

Faced with an unexpected surgery and all that came with it, I had to have something to pull me through. This mantra did that. It helped me lose the weight that I had gained during this time. It helped me finish the book, pushing the final manuscript submission back a few months and understanding that 'embracing the grey', (yet another one of my core strategies) of this opportunity and not being so black and white and not having it happen on the date that I was striving for, for 18 long months, to move this project on to completion allows me to share today that we do have these house rules for a reason. We invite you to stop apologizing for what's not working and accept that there are no excuses only choices.

When you realize your worth, your value and all that you have inside you, you'll understand that you should never give up on yourself. No. Matter. What.

I'm happy to be an illustration of what can happen when you let this mantra work for you. I'm meant to show and share that there is so much in life and even though it gets hard, things will happen when you don't expect them to, they will challenge your thinking. Continue to go for it.

MAVERICK MANTRA

"NOTHING GETS YOU OUT OF STUCK FASTER THAN DOCUMENTING YOUR OWN SUCCESS"

Watch Maverick Video ELEVEN:

Successboarding (1)

Maverick Video TWELVE:

Successboarding (2)

The videos that accompany this Maverick mantra can be found on my YouTube playlist The Making of a Maverick

We can strengthen our 'positive optimistic muscle' through action and visualization by documenting our success. It's proven that the power of visual reminders feeds our motivation for sustained performance and success. Successboarding™ is a self-recognition strategy designed to ignite comprehensive self-reflection cultivating revelations that move you forward.

WHAT IS SUCCESSBOARDING™?

Successboarding™ increases confidence, keeps us positive and documents our success defined as: what's going well, what's feeling good. You'll start to recognize patterns as they emerge. When you document your wins, and look back at them, you'll immediately notice 'patterns' and areas you are recognizing improvement in. You can also use Successboarding™ to get you out of stuck. If you find yourself spinning your wheels but not getting traction you can go to your Successboard™, pick a post-it-note and take that action. This will give you the momentum you need to get over the stagnant hump.

I've studied people and performance and mindset has the biggest impact on how people move forward. Successboarding™ acts as a personal map showing you how you are getting ahead and the types of actions that are getting you there.

When you feed yourself with 'wins and outcomes' vs 'failures or setbacks', you start to become a positive person. Keeping the positives 'top of mind' at all times by consistently documenting, visualizing, visiting, and taking action on these personal wins. When you Successboard™ (stop weekly to document 3 wins/successes), you notice that things really are moving in a forward motion. It sets the tone for thinking positive about your business and how you communicate it to others. You're executing with a 'can do' attitude.

But this strategy is miles more than a visual pick-me-up, it also acts as a compass for self-improvement. As you start to accumulate successes on your Successboard™ you will be able to observe behavioral patterns. These patters act as dynamic insights to how you should focus your time and energy going forward. You can track consistency of actions with this living archive of wins.

You have the answers, that 'personal power', this is a way for you to bring that out. When I realized a need for a more comprehensive analysis of what was working. This is when I took out the post-it's and mocked up my first Successboard™ with this new perspective I was able to remove the numbers and really dial in what actions were working. This is what gave birth to the Successboard™ strategy in 2007.

HERE IS THE FUNDAMENTAL APPLICATION FOR SUCCESSBOARDING™

Each Friday by noon, before you leave for lunch, put 3 post-its down in front of you and write down 3 wins from the week (one per post-it). Now, move these post-it's to your Successboard™, download at www.marlohiggins.com. It's important to write down the month at the top of your Successboard. This is intended as a monthly tracking tool. Once the post-it's are documented and tracked for the month, transfer this Successboard to a 3-ring binder keeping it chronologically. This is how you track and continue to compound the Successboard™ strategy to reference back to. As you go through the month, place your Successboard™ in a high visibility area for you to look at daily and weekly as you navigate and track your wins each week. Keeping this solid system in place, ensures your success.

SUCCESS BY THE NUMBERS:

There are only 20 days of production each month (4 weeks x 5 days a week) and you've documented 12 to 15 'wins/successes' week over week with the goal of finding 3 strong wins each week to document. Why only 3 wins a week? This strategy is intended to keep things light and simple, not feeling like you have to have a win each day, rather pick 3 actions you took that you felt good about, or things that went well that week.

Now compound this strategy over the year, you will have documented up to 156 strong wins/successes in 220 days. Keeping you positive and reminding you of the actions you've taken to gain confidence and increase your performance.

After you've implemented Successboarding™ for a year, take the next step and look back to the same month the previous year and you'll immediately witness growth, because you'll see the types of actions you've taken get bigger and bigger. This naturally happens, because you gain wisdom and experience by doing.

Ask yourself these questions:

» What are these documented wins showing you?

» Why is documenting these wins so powerful?

» What is the value you're receiving by Successboarding™?

It's important to balance the need for self-recognition with a humble attitude and a humble heart. Check your ego and boastful spirit at the door. This is not meant to make you better than anyone else, it's meant to show you that things are going well. This also enhances your personal self-talk and performance. Keeping you from competing with others by assisting you in seeing the power that you have within. This is intended to give you the ability to **"Speak your success, Nothing Less"**, yet another Maverick mantra. Giving you back your 'personal power' a.k.a. self-worth by sharing the positives of what's going well keeping your wins and successes top-of-mind and sharing them in a way that attracts other to you.

"Speak Your Success and Nothing Less"

Successboarding™ positions you with regular wins to set the tone for stronger performance and understanding your self-worth. Go into a job interview or performance review after reminding yourself of these wins. This strategy will give you the ability to be strong and positive helping you to set the tone for a positive conversation by positioning yourself with all that is going well.

Revel in these wins, actions and results. When you can see, I mean visually see this on your Successboard™ it empowers you to keep going and take on bigger things. Speak from a high-level of self-belief. When you believe in yourself, others start to do the same thing. When you position yourself as weak and cowardly, you tend to stay stuck and play small. It's when we feel good about ourselves, our actions, our performance we want to do more. This gives us the fire-in-our-belly to keep going and run our race full on fast!

I also want to elaborate on the purpose of using post-it notes with this strategy, we use them for their simplicity and visual of it. It's not a lot of 'white space' or room to ramble. It's fairly approachable to jot down a quick win on a small space.

Remember, these are *your personal wins*. You're not being judged. If you've had a challenging week, state the obvious, it may be the silliest thing like "made it to the grocery store and fixed a meal", but hey, if that's what felt good to you this week then validate yourself and put it down. This is a tool for you to document YOUR successes, wins, and actions. Just jot it down my friend, you'll be happy you did and remember when you look back, that was something you accomplished that will uplift your spirits and drive your motivation.

WHAT HAPPENS IF YOU CAN'T FIND ANYTHING POSITIVE TO RECOGNIZE?

Again, look back at what I just said about making it to the grocery store. There are no wins or successes too small for this strategy. The purpose is first *documenting*, then you *re-visit* (for fuel), then you look back to *measure* your growth.

I always recommend that we lead by example (be the type of leader others want to follow principal) by sharing your wins and how you've approached them, you immediately become an extension of greater things. Others automatically follow you if you do good things, they see you as a leader taking great actions and they'll simply want to do the same. Share this 'weekly win principal' a.k.a Succcessboarding™ with them, tell them **how** you do it and **why** you do it and invite them to do the same.

THE TEAM SUCCESSBOARDING™ APPROACH

If you're leading a team or an organization, this is one of the greatest ways to get your team focused on the positives. Just imagine what it will feel like when your team of 20 shares, let's say just ONE win they had that week with everyone. Guaranteed, they'll come up with self-recognitions that you had no idea about and now they are even cross-training and sharing things with everyone else that is going well or they are feeling good about. Maybe Cindy-Lou-Who is self-recognizing how she's gotten better at making sales calls. I'd say you invite her to lead a mini-session on opening up doors and how to make effective sales calls. See what I mean? Your team is cross-training and it's all by having them share and recognize themselves in front of others. The cool part as the leader, you simply get to listen and they do all the work and BAM, you've got team synergy happening. These 20 wins can be shared in less than 10 minutes too.

Successboarding™ is genuine self-recognition. These are the things others simply cannot recognize us for. If you're waiting for others to recognize your wins you'll get frustrated. Recognition is one of the most common things lacking in the workplace. This is the purest form of strength and accomplishments that we can share.

This doesn't just work in the realm of business, it works with families too. When I started this concept, our boys were not quite teenagers and it was powerful having them share their wins week over week and recognize things that we never would have seen or heard that they shared.

Introduce this idea to your families, your church friends, the committees you lead, see what happens when you act on this movement of self-recognition.

We all need to be reminded of the good things in life. Be the champion that helps to bring this into the world.

Consistency of Successboarding™ will be the only thing you need to take it a step farther. It's a success principal you'll want to implement into your weekly routine. Adopting this strategy will improve your performance. Find the discipline and consistency to do it.

Write it down.

Visually see it.

Revisit it.

Build off it.

Speak it.

Repetition builds confidence.

Take the consistent action to build yours.

MAVERICK CASE STUDY

GABE ERICKSON, FOUNDER OF FLOW MEDIA INC.

When I aligned the mantra **"everyone wants what I have to offer"**, with Gabe who was fresh out of venture school with his business partners, it immediately increased their company sales. Sharing how to align their thinking to the sale was the first step. This Maverick mantra was not something that was taught to them before, they had to embrace it, making it *their way* of offering their services to others, but first embracing the power of positioning it within their mindset, ensuring their confidence.

To embrace this mantra and ensure its performance for their team, we first had to understand their *type of approach* they wanted to have when offering their business services to others. We drilled down into the types of clients they enjoyed serving. The kind of clients that gave them joy and allowed them to show up and serve, each had these common threads: they gave them FREEDOM to create, TRUST with their approach, their process, their final product and ALLOWED them to do their job.

When these common threads were shared with other prospects that they looked to align with, it started falling into place. They could trust that **"everyone wanted what they had to offer"** because they were certain of the types of folks who would honor their freedom to create, trust them with the final project and fully allow them to operate from their zone. These became their differentiators and allowed them to fully understand who and why **"everyone wanted what they were offering"**. Once this team defined who they were in a way that connected to who they served it was easy to believe this mantra and expand on it to impact sales. When this belief system kicked in and they knew that it was true that **"everyone wanted what they had to offer"** within days they secured new business. Using this mantra matched to what made them different and speaking it at that level in which others could relate to, clearly proved that these differentiators are valuable and position their brand to stand out in the marketplace. Becoming a Maverick is about being bold, different, independent, and eclectic. Bringing all your big beautiful gifts to one place can be hard, but not if you really understand their power.

Gabe shares this;

WHY I CHOSE A CHIEF INSPIRATIONAL OFFICER

The title should perhaps read, "Why I Chose Marlo Higgins," but then again, once I started working with Marlo, I began to realize her title is fully appropriate. I remember sitting down to coffee with her and asking, "What is a Chief Inspiration Officer?"

It turns out, she had fashioned the title for herself. Marlo emanates everything I love about strong leaders--she stays true to her heart and soul.

People ask me, "Is she a business coach?"

"Something like that" is the best I can answer.

I always say the best things in life, the most meaningful and important things, you cannot measure or describe with justice.

How much do I love my family? 10 units? Impossible to say.

Describe the experience of looking out over the Grand Canyon. You can't do it. Words aren't enough. You have to rest in the awe of that moment and trust the experience is sufficient.

And so, it is with Marlo. She is not a business coach. She is not a life coach. She is not a success guru, pouring out mere flatteries for my memorization. She is not formulaic, although she is systematic in her approach.

Before we began working together, I felt as if I were being held to a fire (which is ironic, because she uses fire as a metaphor for igniting success). Fire refines. Fire burns away what we can't shed on our own and allows space for greener, more fruitful life to grow.

That's exactly what happened. She is a catalyst, as fire/heat are in chemical reactions.

I knew I wanted, no needed to be a certain kind of CEO in order to lead my company effectively. Marlo became the amplifier for the voice in my heart that knows what it wants, goes after it, takes risks, lives adventurously, and is sure of itself.

She continues to be the counter to that constant, lying voice that tells me I'm not good enough, that my purpose is out of my reach. We all hear that voice. Some of us may be more honest than others about that, but we all hear it. And it's been an invaluable addition to my life and business to have that booster shot--the fire that reminds me of true things.

When you want to be the best you can be at something, you find the person who can help you get there. Every NFL quarterback that means business has his own coach. Musicians have teachers. Friends have one another.

In order to grow into the man and CEO I wanted to be, I knew I needed Marlo.

But again, there aren't enough words to describe the experience. It's something you must taste and see for yourself.

MAVERICK CASE STUDY

CRAIG MONTZ, ENGINEER

I'm thrilled to share Craig's success because of his passion for communication and leading others. During our time together, I quickly took note of his ability to connect with others with a level of authenticity that naturally motivates. His ability to grow and adapt with his industry is rooted in his desire for continued development of his strengths.

It was clear Craig was ready to move himself into Maverick status. He accepted every challenge I gave him with openness. There were numerous fundamentals that we worked on, (like all clients) but the one that stood out early on, was the area of expectation. As a young professional who had achieved many great wins already in his career, it was important that he also manage the expectations he had of himself through the process of continued growth and achievement.

I think most of us can relate to the importance of both *understanding* and *managing* expectations. I find this often when working with Champions moving into Maverick status, that they can expect so much of themselves and their visions are so big, that it's also important to understand that it takes time to arrive at the end result. To help manage the expectation of time for Craig, we worked on creating a schedule for high-performance as he continued moving himself through this self-development phase. Knowing what to focus on and how to continue to serve within his role and at the same time stretching, growing and achieving.

Craig devoured all the books I recommend for him, he also enjoyed listening to podcasts during his commute time. We shared many recommendations together and still do today. We also hosted Craig on our weekly iTunes podcast series **22 Motivational Minutes with Marlo.**

This was another highlight for me as his coach, I was keenly aware how much he enjoyed learning from others and by having him share his own challenges and wins on our podcast was a great moment for both of us. You can listen to that podcast episode at www.marlohiggins.com.

You'll find value in this episode and learn why Craig chooses to enjoy continued self-improvement and learning.

Here's what Craig shares about his experience, in his words:

A CHANCE ENCOUNTER. (OR LUCK = OPPORTUNITY + PREPARATION)

What can I say? I have sincerely enjoyed my experiences with Marlo since we first met. Two things immediately come to mind when I think back to time spent with Marlo, "Easy to do and easy not to do" and the word "Mantra". Marlo Higgins and I met as we happened to sit at the same table during a key note speaker address at the NextGenSummit 2013. We struck a brief conversation where I learned she provided professional business coaching, something I was in need of. When Marlo invited me to visit with her to discuss the concept of business coaching with her I immediately scheduled a meeting. It was as if fate connected us at the right time in my career.

In the first few minutes during our follow up meeting I could see she was different, well, different than me anyway. Being different was precisely the reason I chose to work with Marlo. She shows up, has" no fear". A significant part of my career has been establishing and growing relationships, this was Marlo's background. Growing relationships is what Marlo does.

Since staring my career, I have seen nothing but change. The first several years of massive growth, followed by the 2008 economic collapse which changed the trajectory of the construction industry. During the period following the economic slowdown I was recruited to lead my employers Cedar Rapids office location. I was in need of a support network as I started the next chapter in my career.

Working with Marlo has expanded my comfort zone increasing my self-confidence. I was frequently living in unfamiliar territory. This was extremely uncomfortable and created high levels of anxiety. Through the coaching assignments and mentoring my comfort zone exponentially expanded. Marlo had the ability to guide me toward the right assignments at the right time... I often found myself reluctantly agreeing with the various assignments we set as she pushed me to the edge. Marlo's technique of follow-up created a high level of self-accountability.

Marlo kept relevant materials in front of me as she pointed me toward readings, practical applications in my daily works, and handouts. Marlo has continued to be available to me as a sounding board at different points in my career. I am proud to say she belongs to my network of coaches.

Execution and results, many individuals talk about results. Marlo demands results are achieved. Several results achieved since first working with Marlo, the size of my immediate family has expanded. I am now an operations manager of a firm pushing $100M in revenue. I am more engaged with the community I work in, regularly attending/organizing functions to recruit youth into the construction career field. My previous employer has successfully increased office revenues by over 20%; we established a satellite office location and set the ground work to begin a second satellite location, increased the number of key operations employees working on our team.

I had a great experience working with Marlo. My comfort zone was expanded, my confidence increased, I received a better understanding of personal and professional branding, found techniques to use in order to help others.

The key strategy for me has been identifying the right things to do and consistently doing them. The right things to do are "easy to do and easy not to do". These words continue to run through my mind. I told Marlo several times I was not into making my own Mantra, so I took up her advice, (kind of) and have been using a phrase to define each year. My favorite has been "Taking consistent action toward definite goals. "My phrase for 2017 is "Implementation, done is better than perfect." My current word for 2017 is "Gratitude". Working with someone helps an individual stay consistent. Even Olympic athletes use a coach!

MAVERICK ACTION

SELF-WORTH

SELF-WORTH. WHAT IS IT? WHY IS IT SO IMPORTANT?

Do you remember watching television or reading a magazine and seeing the words "because I'm worth it"? The slogan was created based on the idea that the consumer should buy the product because they "deserved" it and were worthy of indulging in a beauty product that may not be considered essential. In fact, many companies promote products under the premise that consumers should buy them because they are worthy. This marketing strategy is effective because society in general lacks self-esteem.

Self-worth matters. It matters so much that I've dedicated my time and my brand to promoting its importance. My coaching strategies have developed leaders, brand ambassadors, and all-around business bad-asses. The result of that mission is a multitude of empowered clients.

This process starts by finding the definition of self-worth that works for you.

Ask yourself these questions to begin your own journey to self-worth:

» What is your self-worth?

» Think about what makes you different, and what you bring to the table.

» Create the picture of your own self-esteem.

» Visualize the "destination" version of you. What do you look like at the end of this process?

» What is the picture of yourself when you walk into the room?

» What energy are you bringing?

» How do your talents, value and self-worth (a.k.a. your overall self-esteem) impact what you do and how you do it?

» Why does it matter?

» What's the value for you when you develop this?

» How are you going to use it to serve others?

Be honest with yourself. Figure out the difference between valuing what you have to offer and having an issue with ego. Know that you have what it takes to develop yourself and succeed. How does this idea impact your thinking?

I am all about being able to test and measure success, so I wanted to be sure that my strategies were working, even in an area that can get tough to harvest quantifiable data. Here are four client examples for you. By aligning with these folks, my strategies combined with their hard work, have created these results:

» Took a 3-year marketing company making no more than $42,000 a year and increasing sales to more than $225,000 in less than 6 months.

» Worked with a CEO of a start up to better close business. In just 72 hours he secured more than $90,000+ toward their half-million-dollar 6-month goal.

» Aligned with a CPA to develop systems for higher levels of growth and performance. Business became so healthy that she reported back that she was 'taking business in from a FIREHOSE!' Simply meaning that business really took off.

If you have feelings of self-doubt and a desire to succeed, let these simple, clear strategies go to work for you to immediately take action on to obtain these types of results.

MAVERICK ACTION

TAKE THE STRENGTH FINDERS 2.0 STRENGTHS ASSESSMENT TOOL

Get clear on your strengths (literally). I highly recommend that all my readers and clients take the Strength Finders 2.0 Strengths Assessment tool. It's easy to obtain and extremely valuable (www.strengthfinders. com) to obtain and learn more.

Once you clarify your exact 'strength zone' you'll get out of the gates very quickly. As it mentions in the book *'people have several times more potential for growth when they invest energy in developing their strengths instead of correcting their deficiencies.'*

Maverick Characteristic

Risk

"Take big actions and perform
at your highest level."

MAVERICK CHARACTERISTIC: RISK

I'm going to be honest, it's the area of risk that I enjoy the most. Risk feels scary and hard and exciting to me all at the same time. It's when we step out and take a risk that we really find out about who we are or what's inside of us.

I recently came across an article on Navy seals and it stated that when they feel like they've tapped out during their training exercises and feel that they can't go any further that they've actually only tapped into 40% of their true potential. I think this is why risk feels so big to us. I find this fascinating. Have you ever given up on yourself or your dreams because it just started feeling too hard? I have. I've done it many times. But because I've taken risk multiple times and have pushed with a relentless pursuit to really understand my true grit that I'm always amazed at what comes next, or what I'm able to achieve.

When I reflect and look back at all the actions or the risks I've taken, it gives me great strength every time to keep going and not give up on myself or my dreams. I agree with these Navy seals. It's easy to have that feeling to want to give up, throw in the towel, and stop trying. But what happens when we don't? What if, once you got to this 'giving-up-point', you told yourself "there is still 60% more of me that exists". Now, how do you feel about taking the risk? How does it feel to know that this extra reserve is within you? We have so much inside us that is being underutilized. We're leaving 60% of it on the table when we stop and give up. If we choose not to tap into it, if we choose to never step out and take the risk, we're holding back. We're keeping our potential at bay. Let this empower you to continue to take the risk. Step out of your comfort zone. See what's possible. To me, writing this book feels big and out of my comfort zone, but I'm doing it and it actually feels good, it's something I never thought I would do, but I persevered and continued to work at the process of writing, proving that it was within me. I took a risk.

Others can see the potential in us more than we can see it in ourselves. Why is that? It's because we get in the way of ourselves with our thinking, and we allow fear to creep in, which stops us from believing and taking action. It's in these stretch and challenge zones that we find out what's deep inside us. When we take the risk, we find that reserve tanks been there the whole time. This is that extra amount that Mavericks know exist. When they push farther than they first thought possible, they become unstoppable. Try running fast and fearless like Mavericks do, they embrace the mindset of perseverance and risk. It's pulled me through times when I thought I couldn't do anymore. I continued to run and not let fear deter my potential. Rather, I let the fear be the fuel to get me to the next phase of growth, allowing me to stretch and achieve more than I ever knew that I could.

This is one of the most powerful currency exchanges I have with my clients. It's this extension of power, grit, fuel and fearlessness that they receive when we connect. Synergy to me is everything. Meeting you right where you are. Never judging, but challenging you to be the best you possible.

MAVERICK MANTRA

"CHAMPIONS ARE MOTIVATED BY THE DREAM, AND MADE BY THEIR ROUTINE"

Watch Maverick Video THIRTEEN:

Champions Mantra

The video that accompanies this Maverick mantra can be found on my YouTube playlist The Making of a Maverick

If I write this book but don't *show you how* to create your own mantras, you'll be robbed of the true essence they bring. I've already shared why I adopted mantras now I'd like to share how you can approach creating your own.

It started when I entered into the business of helping others. I was trying to figure out my own journey to success and found a mantra that became my guide. It carried me through and leveraged me to becoming a thought leader and industry expert. From there I began incorporating more mantras into my coaching, helping others find key words and phrases that aligned with what they wanted to accomplish.

I adopted the mantra from <u>Earl Nightingale</u> in 2005; *If you spend an hour of study a day in your chosen field you will be a national expert in 5 years or less.*

I'm a simple girl and don't like to make things complicated. I'm always enamored by watching folks give TED Talks and presentations and doing it from memory. That is why I approached matching all the strategies that I coach on today and position them through easy and memorable Maverick mantras to better remember them and give them the power that they deserve.

When we speak with few words that have impact, they align with power and strength.

I begin creating a mantra by first sitting with the vision and actions I'd like to have happen. Then I align words that match to these visions and actions. I jot them down on post-it notes and let them sit for a bit. I set a defined date and come back to them and select only the top 3-5 that resonate with me.

Once you define what you're striving to achieve, match this vision and definition to words. These words will come together in a way that speak directly to you. Move them around, create and give them power.

You know that my brand mantra is; **"Champions are Motivated by the Dream, and made by their Routine"**.

You can hear all the elements that define what I do and who I am through that simple written truth.

It's a champion's mindset, fueled with motivation on the platform of dreaming of the possibilities and what ifs then consistently doing them. This is why and how I created this mantra to serve my brand. It has power, it's full-bodied and defines all the core values and beliefs that I have around what I do.

We've all heard of New Year's Resolutions, we've all made them but what happens with them? They tend to "go away", why? There is a great tendency to stop being motivated around it if you're not seeing the results you set for yourself.

How can you avoid this and keep consistent motivation?

Create a WORD and a MANTRA for yourself at the beginning of EVERY YEAR, this will allow you to reframe *what you desire* to do *or make happen* that year. Words and Mantras are two different things but both have HUGE IMPACT on how you sustain your success all year long.

In my opinion, this is the MOST VALUABLE action you can take to set you up for a great year.

It's simple... reflect in a quite space that allows you to fuel your desires and energy. This could be at the gym while working out or maybe it's in the kitchen while cooking a great meal, just allow yourself to think of the BEST WORD to describe your *up-coming* YEAR. What *type of year do you want to have* and *what is the feeling you want* to have around it?

Here's an example for you:

My WORD in 2012 was DETERMINED! This ONE WORD framed my entire year. I was DETERMINED to be a great wife, a great mother, a great friend, this list goes on. I was DETERMINED to build a great brand and serve my clients with value. I was DETERMINED to make it, I was DETERMINED to grow, learn, ask, achieve and receive. Anyone who interacted with me in 2012 would validate and probably tell you that I approached EVERY THING I did that year with determination.

My MANTRA in 2012 was: Champions are motivated by the dream and made by their routine! The reason I selected a mantra like this was 1) it was an Olympic year, so a lot of energy went towards fueling champions and watching them that summer 2) knowing that in order to be a TOP CHAMPION we have to have a GREAT ROUTINE that allows that to happen. You can't just start lifting weights on Monday and by Friday of the same week be the WORLDS CHAMPION weight lifter, right? It's the routine of those daily actions in the gym that allows that build up to gain traction. Ah, routines, systems and organization! It gives us clarity and a path to follow.

WHY MANTRAS?

I've found that if I'm not "feeling it" or start to wane that all I have to do is speak my WORD and MANTRA and that re-frames me to keep going, stay on task, and seek out new challenges. I say to myself "Marlo, get going because you are DETERMINED to do IT today (whatever *it* is that I'm trying to do), this week, this month" ... can you see how this can relate to your success? Can you hear the value of it? We all need "tools, tips and resources" to move forward or get ahead, this is one of many tips for you Maverick. My personal challenge to you is to create this for yourself.

To keep this example going for you to see its value, *My WORD in 2013 was RADIATE* – I had to simply "show up" and radiate all that year with what I had to offer. You can already hear that my determination and champion mindset set in 2012 set me up to radiate and ooze gratitude in 2013. That's the cool part, this strategy compounds itself.

Let me share my last 8 years of words and mantras with you so you can see how I approached my growth and feelings toward the coming year and how by choosing each year carefully, it can actually set you up for the coming year.

Year	WORD	MANTRA
2010	**SOLUTION**	You'll figure it out.
2011	**SURVIVE**	A setback is a setup for a comeback.
2012	**DETERMINED**	Champions are motivated by the DREAM but made by their ROUTINE.
2013	**RADIATE**	Ask, Believe, Achieve, and Receive with Gratitude.
2014	**OPEN**	Make me useful and be open to receive.
2015	**S-T-R-O-N-G**	Spread good energy and pay it forward.
2016	**CALM**	Run fast, live fearless.
2017	**IMPACT**	Be Transparent and Make an Impact.

Here's this year's word and mantra;

2018	**BREAKTHROUGH**	Do One Thing Every day that Scares You

You can see, feel, and hear the pattern. Year over year, **each core focus of intention** set me up for amazing momentum, energy and success. It works!

I always say that what we do is an extension of who we are. By creating your mantra and defining your annual word, it allows you to stay focused with clarity toward the type of year you'd like to have and ensures consistency with how to approach it. Let's say that you get six months into the year and somehow you get off track. Going back and using your mantra to reset and reframe will help you immediately get moving forward again. If you find any kind of doubt or scarcity creep in, your mantra has the ability to serve you and help you remember what you chose, and why you chose it.

Don't overthink this process. Allow yourself to create just the right word and mantra that will serve you each year. Then, run your race full on fast for the next 365 days and stay true to the mantra that you created. Get to the end of the year then reflect back on what it did for you and why it was so powerful. Do this during the time you're getting ready to start creating your new upcoming mantra for the coming year.

Go a step further and keep track of them so you can reflect back to see your years compounded and if you stayed on course for the year or use it as a guide to help you get back to where you were headed to begin with.

You've got the power and the answers within you. It starts with desire, then matching it to actions to get the results you'd like to achieve.

Maverick Mantra

"You Can't Try and Fail at the Same Time, It's Impossible"

Watch Maverick Video FOURTEEN:

Self-Belief (potato and straw)

The video that accompanies this Maverick mantra can be found on my YouTube playlist The Making of a Maverick

I've spent a lot of time speaking about the power of confidence and how necessary it is to remove self-doubt in order to be successful. However, I believe that in order for you to understand the power that lies in letting go of doubt, you need to understand that sometimes your doubt is founded. Sometimes giving up is all you can do. But just because you gave up on one idea doesn't mean that it's over.

I'd like to elaborate on why this mantra exists and how to leverage it to work for you. If you think about it, it really is impossible to TRY and FAIL at the SAME time. As long as your trying, you're not failing. You may try things that don't work, but it's ok, I know that you're learning by trying. It takes multiple tries sometimes to get it right, but that is where Maverick status comes from. Mavericks don't give up and they don't give in. They continue to try and make things happen. It's this ferocious tenacity that comes into play when leveraging from a Champion to a Maverick in status. Mavericks have the vision that anything is possible. You have to have this to succeed in business and in life.

As someone who has helped to start a company, rebrand another and launch my own, let's just say that I've failed multiple times through each of these experiences. It is through those failures that I continued trying and making whatever wasn't work, work. It's one of the reasons that I can bring this book to you and share these mantras, because they were created though my failures. I simply documented what I was trying to accomplish, when it worked, I detailed how I approached the success and made it one of my life's purposes to share them with others so they too can pivot and move through the path to higher levels of achievement by using these Maverick mantras to strengthen their positive, 'I can do anything' mindset to achieve.

During trying times, I often read this excerpt from the book; The Law of Divine Compensation, by Marianne Williamson (if you don't have it, get it today!)

Dear God,

I surrender to You who I am, what I have, and what I do. May my life and talents be used in whatever way serves You best. I surrender to You my failures and any pain still in my heart. I surrender to You my successes and the hopes that they contain. May the Light of Your Love shine deep within my heart and extend through me to bless the world.

Amen.

A SETBACK IS A SETUP FOR A COMEBACK

Through numerous trials, obstacles and setbacks I've had to fuel myself up with sayings that motivate and inspire me. Like you, I've read a lot of books and spend most of my time learning from others and how they've moved through their failures to achieve great success. You've heard me say, no one is immune to trying times. It's going to happen. We've all experienced them and there will be more to come, that's a guarantee. The best part is, these setbacks if looked at with power can serve you.

Give this mantra a try; tell yourself that **'A setback is a setup for a comeback'**. Knowing that what you may be experiencing, can also teach you one of your greatest lessons. It may actually be the thing that gets you further just by experiencing it. The power within this mantra is incredible. Take a setback that you've experienced and let it leverage you for a setup. Let it go to work for you. Let it teach you something, or show you that it may feel like failure right now, but when you look back it may also be one of your biggest setups for achievement in life.

I had one of these catalyst setbacks in 2010 with my health, but without that experience, I guarantee that I would not be sharing with you from my own brand perspective today. That setback allowed me to take myself out of the game (professionally) for an entire year and allowed me the time to get crystal clear on how I wanted to serve, what value I wanted to share with others and how I would approach sharing that value.

My brand and my title came from my biggest setback. I was diagnosed with my first tumor that year, a brain tumor. If you've followed Scott Hamilton or Cheryl Crow, we have similar benign brain tumors. Instead of letting that derail me and kick me to the curb of life's achievements, I used this mantra as my way of getting through that tough time. Since then however, I've experienced numerous other benign tumors throughout my body having multiple surgeries to remove them. But I gained strength and power through each of these personal triumphs. I'm known to say "that I am the healthiest, unhealthy person you'll ever meet". I use this to make light of these setbacks because there's not a dang thing I can do about them. There's nothing that I'm doing to cause them, they just happen. These experiences help to make me a Maverick. These setbacks, these failures in life and business, all of this makes me stronger, and allows me to say that I'm a tumorlicious badass!

I continue to try and don't allow myself to fail. I continue to put one foot in front of the other, lean on my fearless spirit and constant drive and continue to align to powerful people doing powerful things which allow me to get swept up in this tsunami of positive and powerful actions.

We don't always get to choose what happens to us, but we do get to choose how we'll frame ourselves and the actions we'll take to get through them.

A LOOK INTO MY MINDSET OF MAVERICKS AND CHAMPIONS:

(this section is based on speech excerpts)

More than anything I love champions. Mavericks. Thoroughbreds. The best of the best. The top 4% like my favorite book, <u>The Slight Edge</u> by Jeff Olson.

Why, champions? They challenge me. They show me that its possible. Anything's possible. They prove that if you work at it. You can have it. We simply need to connect to our discipline strength and a champions mindset to become fearless (in business and in life).

When we're fearless, we surrender. When we surrender, we have no fear. When we have no fear. We have the ability to take action. I've had to face my fears more than once. When I simply surrender to whatever is coming, whatever is happening I'm able to accept it in a way that's empowering.

I love to be empowered. I actually LOVE these four core feelings; peaceful, energized, empowered and love. I make every decision from 'how I want it to feel'. I ask myself 'does this feel peaceful?', is this energizing? Am I empowered? When I operate from this depth of my core, I know it's right. It's pure. It has intention.

I surrender to my fear. I allow rather than resist.

I've been shown, through numerous obstacles and barriers of my own that it can happen. I'm "just a girl" and the powerful and amazing people that I've been able to align with have superseded my expectations. All my life, I've been enamored by influence and power.

I love power. I guess I see power as strength. I need strength, more often than not. So, to align with powerful opportunities, powerful people, powerful initiatives, it simply gives me strength.

Like you, nothing comes easy. I never go for easy, I'm driven by challenges, obstacles and barriers. The power I've 'harnessed' through the witness of champions allows me to bypass easy and step into the 'let's go for it, why not' mindset. I always say 'the magic's in the stretch zone'. I choose to stretch every day and see what happens when I do. I've achieved more than I would have if I would have chosen to stay small, comfortable, not stretching. Empowering. That's a choice. If I'm empowered, I can empower others.

My product is people. I'm called on to challenge people to develop their 'personal power', defined as their value, talents and self-worth. When we tap into this personal power, we understand the depth of our being. We gain confidence, we become better at leading ourselves and ultimately others. When we do this, we perform at higher levels. When we perform at high levels we achieve more, we do more, we become more. I've always wanted more for myself. I want more for others. That's just me being me!

When you impact someone by developing them as a champion, we all win.

I love champions, I love people, I love power, I love performance but for all the right reasons.

It's no mistake that my final closing Maverick Action is around destressing and removing overwhelm so you can get back to being yourself. It's a must for all of us. It's important to create a way to 'dial-down' and relax ourselves so we can enjoy and be present, sweet and gentle. I strive to create an environment both personally and professionally described as a 'soft-place-to-land'. It's just right to have a soft landing at the end of the day, or the end of the week. If you choose to run fast daily in pursuit of your dreams and be a Maverick or a champion, it's just as important to have a way to dial back and just be yourself.

MAVERICK ACTION

SWEATSHIRT | SHOWER | PIZZA

Watch Maverick Video FIFTEEN:
Sweatshirt | Shower | Pizza – 3 Grounding Tools

The video that accompanies this Maverick action can be found on
my YouTube playlist The Making of a Maverick

WHAT ARE 3 THINGS THAT WOULD CONSISTENTLY UNWIND YOU?

It's more than just 'things' though. It has to be actions you can take that allow you to remove stress and settle into being peaceful. For this to work, you've got to create physical actions to take, a series of movements that allow you to remove the stress.

I adopted and took actions on this in my early twenties, when I was feeling overwhelmed and stressed. A sweatshirt, shower and a pizza were my "go-tos" to get back to feeling better and relieving my stress. It became clear that this was a powerful combo that I consistently turned to when that feeling arose. It was my way of putting an action to what I needed to have happen. Looking back, it's seems weird that early on in my life I was adopting principles that I coach on today. That just makes it clearer to me that I am meant to do what I am doing professionally and it's by my personal experiences that allows this natural talent to shine.

So, why shower, sweatshirt and pizza?!? Well, I guess the shower simply to "wash away" the ick of the day. The sweatshirt because it's just so b-a-s-i-c and comfy and pizza because it is simply cheap comfort food. I refer to being GROUNDED and CONSISTENT. This stems from a simple ritual that has lasted many years and I am still proud that I know how to destress myself and get back to remembering what matters – my sanity and the feeling of comfort.

It's by no surprise that our family has personally adopted this strategy! You will find us ordering pizza EVERY Friday night. Now that our boys are grown and independent, they still find themselves with their friends ordering pizza on Friday nights. It's an easy thing to do, it removes the 'expectation' of what we should do or what we should eat. You simply slide in sideways from your week and have peace and enjoy. You can stop thinking and start relaxing. You deserve that.

I challenge you to create 3 things that will ground you back to feeling better about your day and give you the comfort you require to be WHOLE again. Of course, healthy vices, my friend!

MAVERICK CASE STUDY

AMANDA LUND, BRAND STORYTELLER

Where would I be without 'Miss Amanda'? it's easy to put her in the 'risk category' of things and let me share why.

Amanda has been a catalyst to who I am today with our brand. She's been with me from inception and quickly became a prominent member of 'Team Marlo' (she titled that by-the-way). It has taken us years to arrive where we are today. It's no mistake the pivots and divots we've made along the way. We quickly realized we had that *synergy* that was necessary to keep pushing and make the climb. No. Matter. What. Even when resistant forces told us otherwise, we refused to listen and chose to beat to our own drum and make our way as Mavericks. I see Amanda as a Maverick and I'm sure she'd say the same about me.

Our alignment happened extremely organically and the way I like to see things happen, without force and with complete purity. I'm sure that's why it works every time. I let bigger forces take the lead on the things in life that are bigger than me. Things like my client base, my health, our family's happiness, all those big things that we simply cannot control. Like I tell my clients, "if we are truly meant to align with this format, then it's meant to be".

I've witnessed the growth of Amanda and how she's completed her degrees, submitted writing proposals, trained herself to do things she didn't know how to do, continued to write her own book (a novel), all the while, championing through being a wife, mother, daughter, sister, friend and so much more.

Throughout the years of making things happen with my brand and at the same time experiencing health setbacks, Amanda would not let anything fall through the cracks. During those times when I simply could not write the blog, or submit the article she stepped in and did it. Amanda quickly learned a very important principle from me: INITIATE. I refer to it as the sexiest word in business. Initiate an idea, a plan, a solution, a strategy, whatever it is, just initiate. Take the risk, step outside of the box and go for it. A lot more can happen when you do vs. staying stuck or playing small. Amanda never let me play small. She kept the challenge alive for me and continued to bring the value when I couldn't. I think you can better understand now how I chose to put her into the risk category of becoming a Maverick. Of course, there were days when we weren't feeling or acting like Mavericks, but those days proved to us that we could, and here we are now, sharing it with others.

You hear me say "I'm just a girl". No more special than anyone else, but sometimes when we align with someone who can challenge us, and stretch us to bigger visions of tomorrow allows us to realize, maybe we are more. We have greater value, and that is a small sampling of how Amanda has done this for me personally. I'm forever grateful to her.

Here is what Amanda has to say from her perspective, remember, she's a writer, and I love the approach she took to share;

A LETTER TO MY PRE-MARLO SELF

Dear Amanda (circa 2011),

I have to be honest with you, there's work ahead.

I hear you practicing small talk under your breath and double-checking your good shirt for baby spit-up. You're late for a networking meeting.

I know those nerves, the way your arms feel floaty without a baby cradled within them. I have some seemingly bad news for you. It only gets harder from there.

I know your brain – because it's my brain too. I know that every time you've been presented with an opportunity there's been a safety response that's triggered deep within those synapses. Don't do it. It's the neurons, or evolution, or something. Just keep doing what you're doing – it's safer that way.

That's not your fault. In a few years, you'll learn that our brains are wired to keep us safe and we only have a few seconds to override the "safety" in favor of those choices that make us grow. It's an eye-opener, but it's not the beginning.

That networking meeting is the beginning – the moment when you begin the path that will lead to me – the writer, the entrepreneur – the version of us that's six years and a million lifetimes away.

You'll make the decision to stay after that meeting and speak with Marlo for the first time. Then you'll override that "safety" and deviate from the sales pitch, admitting your love of writing. That's it, Self – that is the beginning.

That admission will lead to a conversation that will lead to a writer's workshop, that will lead to a night class at the community college, that will lead to an Associate's Degree. From there, you'll attend more workshops. You'll write blogs. You'll write a manuscript. People will ask you to write for websites. You'll graduate with honors from the University of Iowa. You'll write and cry and fail and lose clients and gain better ones and celebrate as you see your name in print for the first of many times.

Then, believe it or not, you'll have a team and a brand message of your own – teaching others how to write with authenticity in a world of digital noise. You'll help businesses put their "why" into words, and all because you chose to believe the woman who sat across from you at a Mexican restaurant and told you it was not only possible, it was inevitable.

So, when Marlo tells you she believes in you, go home and kiss your baby. Whisper in his ear that big things are happening. He'll believe you, Self – but only because whether you've realized it or not – you've started to believe it too.

Love Always,

Amanda (circa 2017)

End Note;

Coaching is personal development. Each of us is unique and different and in honor of each of these clients I share in this book, I choose to stand with integrity and share only what is necessary for you to understand why these clients chose to develop into Maverick and Champion status and the approach we took to get there. I give you what you need and if you desire more, you can reach out through the contact page on my website at www.marlohiggins.com to connect with me directly.

This book and these case studies are intended to give you a flavor of what we do and what's been achieved. That's different for all of us. I trust you understand and will honor this.

A NOTE TO FINISH STRONG

When faced with adversity, do you lie down or do you fight?

Do you make the most of each day?

What will your legacy be?

When adversity strikes, it's not what happens that determines our destiny, it's how we react.

You have to believe you can do something and then have the courage and determination to see it through.

In closing, when our boys were younger, I would check in with them by asking this question; "are you a lover or a fighter?" One always said, "I'm a lover mom" and the other one "I'm a fighter".

I relate to the fighter spirit. It's this bold persona that I write this book on Making Mavericks and building Champions.

I've gone to great depths to figure out why I'm a fighter and what the value is behind this innate quality. I was born with a fighter's instinct for a reason. At age 12, I knew that I would be called upon to be a professional encourager in life. This early realization resulted in my current position as a Chief Inspirational Officer. It's no mistake that this is my title. The challenges and triumphs that I've endured and experienced have allowed me the ability to inspire and motivate others to reach their fullest potential.

My problems are infinitely small compared to most, but each come with their own grit to overcome and achieve. They've each taught me something different. I've had to accept and learn from all of them in their own way, during their own time and on their own terms. I never asked for any of it, but I now realize, that by accepting them and embracing and never fearing why or what, but being open to them, that's allowed me to be who I am today.

I trust that this book served you for a reason. There was something that you read or a story you heard that resonated with you. Take that as fuel to make things happen in your world. I challenge you now to never sit on the sidelines. To always get into the game of life and business, but do it in a way where you can trust yourself, the process, and the end result. My final message to you is this - you have all the answers. They are there. They are waiting for you to tap into them so you can better understand their existence and the reason for them. Release them. Enjoy them. Embrace them. Own them, but for God's sake, do something with them!

With deep, deep, gratitude I thank you for giving this book your time. That means a lot to me. After all, I wrote it for you.

XO,

Marlo

THE MAVERICK MOVEMENT

#MAVERICKMOVEMENT

I started the **#MaverickMovement** to create momentum, synergy, community, and interaction. It's meant to be a powerful experience that challenges you with key questions asked daily throughout the year that assist you to solve problems in the key areas of performance and learning within our community.

First, take the **#MaverickMovement** challenges by asking yourself the key questions.

Then share the **#MaverickMovement** challenge questions with your team members, organizations, peers and colleagues. Go even further, and involve your family and community.

There is power in awareness.

By challenging yourself with key questions to answer, and challenged with actions to take, the momentum will arm you in creating performance momentum.

You read about performance and the various Maverick mantras you can speak, to set up your champions mindset.

You've read about taking action to develop towards Maverick status.

Now you have the tools to be a part of it. I invite you to bring the Maverick Mindset to serve a greater good, here's how:

Follow the **#MaverickMovement** online.

You will find us active and responding on Instagram, LinkedIn and my favorite, Twitter. Visit each, and like, join me, and participate, comment, and share with others. You are a brilliant Maverick. Spread your voice, we want you to be a part of it.

Let's Make More Mavericks Together!

A Tweetable Quote;

Never go for easy, be driven by your challenges, obstacles and barriers.

– Marlo Higgins

Each one of the Maverick case studies in the book has a blog written about them, a podcast interview to listen to on 22 Motivational Minutes with Marlo, and a video interview to watch. They can be found on our website www.marlohiggins.com under the Blog, Podcast, and Video tabs.

ACKNOWLEDGMENTS

I am invincible, unbreakable
Unstoppable, unshakeable
They knock me down, I get up again
I am the champion
You're gonna know my name
You can't hurt me now
I can't feel the pain
I was made for this, yeah, I was born to win
I am the champion

Carrie Underwood, "Champion"

GRATITUDE

This is my first time at having the opportunity to write an acknowledgements section after having just completed the last page of the manuscript. I'm extremely blessed and immensely grateful that so many people have inspired me, challenged me and supported me through this process.

It starts with my mama, the infamous '**Grandma D**', who as a single parent happened to raise two accomplished kids. I realize it wasn't an easy feat, but again, nothing good ever is.

My exclusive Maverick tribe of clients who hired me to challenge and serve them. It was through our synergy that assisted in bringing all of this to life.

Amanda Lund, my wingwoman, who helped me through the days and times when I just couldn't make it happen. She showed up *every time* and made sure it did.

Justin Sachs, my publisher and the founder of Motivational Press, from our first call who believed in me and consistently held me to the vision and guaranteed me we'd do whatever it takes. We did, and I'm grateful.

Mark Brodinsky, my personal motivator and friend and who I know will someday impact the lives of a billion people. You always knew what type of motivational push I needed at just the right time.

Catherine Saykaly-Stevens our Social Media Consultant and trainer who stepped in during the eleventh hour to guide us through the social media fog. We learned a lot and know that so much more is coming.

For contributing directly to this work, I am grateful for **James Klein** watching me present one day then asking to learn more. To **Craig Montz** who happened to sit next to me at lunch during a conference and now years later getting to share more of who you are and why you do what you do. **Gabe Erickson**, who always makes my light shine. Your faith is unmeasurable. You have the vibrato of Goliath, the biblical warrior. To **Alison Turner**, a true soul-friend who always showed up for me no-matter-what. For **Carissa Kruse**, who was never afraid of the challenge. To **Aaron Proietti**, Founder of Adaptivity Enterprises, LLC who divinely showed up to the table and had the genius to turn my desire of an assessment into reality. I give you all the credit.

I've got to mention **'The Six Pack Chiquita's'**, my powerful and personal tribe of best friends who made me laugh when I needed to, and never allowed me to take myself too seriously. Thank you, Miss Kim, Traci, Julia, Shannon and Tracie.

My true love, **Scott,** my rock who never lets me fall. Your steadfast support in my life cannot be described. You are an amazing husband and father to our two boys. Thank you, we appreciate you.